Church on Trial

Jessica Rose

DARTON·LONGMAN+TODD

Many people have generously shared their stories in the making of this book. All names have been changed for the purposes of writing about their experiences.

First published in 2009 by
Darton, Longman and Todd Ltd
1 Spencer Court
140–142 Wandsworth High Street
London SW18 3EU

© Jessica Rose

The right of Jessica Rose to be identified as the author of this work has been asserted in accordance with the Copyright, Designs and Patents Act 1998

ISBN 978-0-232-52768-1

A catalogue record for this book is available from the British Library.

Phototypeset by Kerrypress Ltd, Luton, Bedfordshire
Printed and Bound in Great Britain by Athenaeum Press, Gateshead, Tyne & Wear

Church on Trial

For Father Tom Stevens, a true friend in need

Contents

1 Putting the church on trial 1

Trying it on for size 9
2 To go or not to go – what draws us to church? 11
3 The 'service-provider' and the community: a question of hospitality 29

How is the church behaving in people's lives? 41
4 Witnesses for the defence 43
5 Witnesses for the prosecution 63
6 When the event is mightier than the structure 85
7 What is it all for? 105
8 The body broken 119

What does it mean to be church? 137
9 The problem of the 'feel-good factor' 139
10 Living within the wounds of Christ's body 151
11 A gospel of encouragement 165

Notes 187
Index 190

1

Putting the church on trial

> It's like church – you think maybe if you go,
> the faith will be given, but it isn't. It has to be
> there already in you, I guess. Or maybe you
> have to persevere.[1]

When asked if they would be willing to be interviewed for this book people have often responded by having a great deal to say – positive and negative – about their experiences of church life. Others have asked, 'Why bother? – the churches are on their way out.' These people, too, have interesting things to say.

We live in an age where 'church' is no longer a given in society, even where Christianity is the dominant religion. Many would even question whether, in order to be a Christian, it is necessary to belong to any kind of church, and vast numbers of people, while convinced of the importance of the spiritual dimension of our lives, choose to stay away from any kind of institutionalised religion or even belief system. Yet some things do not go away. In all kinds of ways – through nature, through scientific exploration, art, music, human relationships and personal crisis – people find themselves in touch with a level of experience that is not accounted for by the physical senses. At this level of experience people find themselves in touch with connections that transcend not only space but also time. And some people can only make sense of it by naming it as the source of all our being, as God.

Even this does not necessitate signing up to any religious institution. Yet many people also feel a deep need to share their spiritual experience with others, and to share prayer and meditation, as well as a need for a faith community. Spiritual exploration is not only difficult to begin, but is in itself risky, liable to take us to places we do not understand and where we no longer understand ourselves. Here the experience and received wisdom of a faith community can be of great help, as well as ritual and tradition, especially when it comes to major events in our lives. And, in a fragmented society, many people have a powerful need for a sense of belonging.

In search of these things, some people find their way in – or back in – to our churches, and there are of course many within those churches who have never left. Nevertheless, churchgoing is no longer the norm. Churchgoers find themselves at odds with society, and even among the spiritually aware, to be a church member is something of a curiosity. In a radical reversal that has taken place over the last half century, it is now churchgoers who are the strangers in society – not those who have rebelled or fallen away. In a sense this is a marvellous opportunity for the churches to shed a great deal of cultural and historical baggage and get back to basics. The perceived irrelevance of the churches offers a new freedom simply to *be* church – but what is the experience of people who go to church in search of something they cannot find elsewhere? And how does that experience relate to what people perceive the church to be?

For the purposes of this book, 'the church' does not refer to any particular church. It is taken to mean the Christian churches – Western and Eastern – who profess the Trinity and the incarnation, regard themselves as the Body of Christ, and celebrate the Eucharist. It is assumed in this book that all the Christian churches, fragmented though they are in practice, are deeply united in their attempt to be the Body of Christ on earth. This does not mean we should ignore the differences, but for our purposes we can lay them aside.

What is important here is how people experience life within the churches and how that relates to the common enterprise. The Christian churches are full of people who find themselves at odds with the societies in which they live, at odds with each other, and often at odds with the very institutions to which they belong. However much the churches may differ in their doctrines and their rituals, it is clear that the problems – and the joys – that people experience take place throughout all kinds of church life.

In an age where churchgoing is largely a matter of conscious choice, however, it is sometimes easier to see why people leave than why they stay. Some leave through inertia – church simply loses significance for them; others because of a painful clash of loyalties. They find that what the church believes – or appears to believe – about the way we should live is incompatible with their own understanding of themselves or those they love. A common experience is that of Helen Reed in David Lodge's novel, *Thinks*, who was brought up as a Catholic, but abandoned the practice of her faith during her second term at Oxford, 'at the same time that I lost my virginity. The two events were connected,' she says. 'I could not with sincerity confess as a sin something I had found so liberating, or promise not to do it again.'[2] Some have stopped going to church because of a loss of ritual ('There is no difference between what goes on here and a football match or a barbecue') – and others because of too much ('How can we spend all this time in church putting so much energy into services when we are paying no attention to the suffering of the people around us – or indeed to our own families or children?'). From either perspective one can ask, 'Where is God in all this?'

The church is a complex organism, made up of popes and patriarchs as well as parish priests, bishops, monks and nuns, and members of local congregations; among these we find the people who hold it altogether, and people on the fringes. It is also a mystical body, including those who have died as well as the living, and the interface of all this in the worship where we also find music, words, tradition, teaching. To some the church is a building on the street corner, or a particular community; to others it is something that extends, and connects people, across the boundaries of space and time.

What does it mean, then, to put the church on trial – an enterprise that can seem at best hubristic, at worst useless? What possible significance can there be to any outcome? As well as asking what goes on within the churches, we also perhaps have to ask ourselves what the church is for. This is a reasonable question in an age when to the majority of the population it appears irrelevant, if not positively unhelpful or even decadent. To some extent we can describe particular functions that the church needs to fulfil. Yet ultimately there is no answer. It is an assumption of this book that the church, however fragile, fragmented and diminished, simply *is*. In that sense it is a trial without a verdict. What we can do, however, is ask what people are looking for in the church, and what the church does: we can ask in what ways it is possible to discover within it a Christ-centred community – how it reveals itself as the Body of Christ. In exploring this we will draw on conversations with people who have different kinds of relationship with the church: regular members, occasional visitors, and those who actively keep away. It is not a survey or a statistical analysis, but an attempt to identify some expectations and quality of experience. We will not be attempting to address the large questions that affect church life today, except in so far as they affect people's experience on the ground.

The resulting 'trial' can be interpreted in three different ways.

The first is in relationship to the marginal nature of church in our society. While there are still a great many people for whom belonging to a church is as natural as breathing, the church is constantly 'on trial' by a proportion of its members in the same way that, say, a carpet sample might be, when it is brought home to see if it suits the décor. Many churchgoers – and this is a process that can go on for years at a time – can be said to be trying church out, trying it on for size. Do I like this or not? Does it meet my needs? Is it being what I think church should be? Does it make any difference to my life? Is it worth it?

Secondly, we can put the church on trial by asking how it is behaving, and whether it is in any recognisable sense being church – as opposed to a club or community centre, or even, perhaps, a repository for traditionalists. How does its behaviour relate to what we find in the gospels, and what part is it playing in society? There is no denying that most of the churches are in a bad way: their hymns and traditions are forgotten – or indeed never even learned by anyone under forty – their sacraments a curiosity, poorly understood. Is it not simply cruel to place on trial something that is already crumbling, wounded, torn apart by its own disease? Yet, the church, whether it likes it or not, is the Body of Christ. As that

Body, can it facilitate enlargement of soul, bring us closer to God individually and collectively – or is it doomed to shrinkage?

The third and most important aspect of our trial involves an exploration of what we bring – as human beings – to the body itself.

The idea for the title of this book came from a book by Rowan Williams, *Christ on Trial* (London: Fount, 2000), in which an archbishop (at that time, of Wales) challenges Christians of all kinds to identify their own process in the events surrounding the trial and crucifixion of Christ. These Gospel stories, he reminds us, reveal to us 'the dilemma of our own violence'. For most of us, he concludes, 'the decisions are not ... issues that are instantly and obviously ones of life and death, but are rather gnawing anxieties about whom to believe and how to put the right questions to ourselves' (p. 35).

Faced with the violent disagreement, rivalry, corruption and sense of impending doom that characterises so much of church life today, we will be drawing on people's everyday experience of the churches to ask what some of those 'right questions' might be. In a sense this is an extension of the 'Christ on Trial' project begun in Jerusalem two thousand years ago. If the churches are the Body of Christ on earth, if they in some sense represent his continuing incarnation, our current trial is closely bound up with that historical one.

In thinking about church life, we will not be concerned with trying to solve the huge questions that face the churches today as they grapple with contemporary culture. Nor will we have much to say about the larger role of church in society. Our main concern is with what goes on at the level of individuals, their experiences and responses, rather than at the institutional level.

Finally, it is only reasonable in a book of this kind, which is rooted in people's experience, to say something about the background of the author. I grew up, as it were, on an island – an urban island surrounded not by water but by roads. It contained the vicarage in which we lived, the church of which my father was vicar, the parish hall, and a garden. All this was bounded by brick walls and hedges, beyond which lay a prosperous London suburb.

Through the gates and into the house and the church came large numbers of people: parishioners, beggars, visiting bishops and, only occasionally, friends. The cycle of church services and parish life governed our lives. There was much that was good about this, and much that was not. Like many vicarage children we felt constantly on show, like royalty, and it is difficult to find one's own relationship to church or to faith in these circumstances.

Like so many vicarage children, my brother and I shook the dust of church from off our feet when we left home. He developed a deep and personal spirituality, which for most of his life did not include church, though years later when he was dying, thanks to a true and loyal priest, he received communion often. I myself did not simply reject the church – for many years I *forgot* it. I forgot it so profoundly that when my father died, I could think of no way to explain to my 4-year-old daughter what had happened, except that death was the end of life, and Grandpa was now dead. We both found this depressing. I went through the funeral – a requiem Mass in the church where he had been priest and I had been organist throughout my teens – in a kind of trance, having at least had the wisdom to refuse to play the organ for it (as I had done for the funerals of all my grandparents). Only several weeks later did a startling thought occur to me, and I said to my daughter, 'By the way, some people believe that when you die you go to heaven.' 'What's heaven?' she asked, and this led to talk of God.

For me, this was the beginning of looking for a community with whom I could share the search for God, and a growing desire to pray. Being an organist, it was easy to 'try out' various churches by making myself available to play for services when regular organists were on holiday. This was a good way to take part in services while at the same time maintaining a certain detachment. Sometimes I was impressed by what I saw, the sincerity with which certain communities approached worship, and the way they talked afterwards. Sooner or later, however, I would catch a glimpse of familiar attitudes, of parish life, and quickly absent myself. For several years I attended the Eucharist at an Anglican convent where the nuns were contemplatives. It was for a time the perfect solution, providing a community that shared with me deeply at a spiritual level, and required very little at any other. To this day I do not know the names of most of these sisters, though I regard them as my friends.

One July Sunday in the late 1980s, seeking to integrate worship more closely with my ordinary life, I attended the Orthodox liturgy in a thriving church very close to my home. I was overcome by a sense of alienation and left half way through. A few months later I went back, and was equally overwhelmed by a sense of homecoming, and that is where I have been ever since. Such is the strange nature of our journeys. It was a peculiar and unnerving moment when, having grown up in a vicarage, at the age of thirty-eight I sat down with a priest for the first time to talk about myself. Becoming a member of the Orthodox Church was not a dogmatic decision on my part and had nothing whatever to do with the ordination of women or other cultural issues in Anglicanism. It was simply the place where, liturgically, I felt at home, and in whose liturgical and theological tradition I found enormous richness. This sense of homecoming has been greatly tested not only by a volatile parish life, but also by the wider scene of international church politics, which has had a huge effect on our local communities. While this is not my core concern here, this experience will inevitably inform my approach to the subject of this book.

Like people, churches change: they grow or become stuck, they can become ill, they can demonstrate amazing capacity for regeneration. In thinking about my own relationship with the church, I am reminded of a comment made by someone who had been (happily) married for thirty years: 'The strange thing is, the longer you are together, the closer you become, the more you realise how other, how different from yourself, the other person is.' There is no abiding city – yet it can be argued that for a Christian, the church cannot be second guessed. It abides as Christ's Body on earth until the end of time.

It is sometimes noted, especially by people who are very familiar with the churches, that people within them seem to behave less well, and with less common humanity, than those outside. This is a puzzle to which we shall return. At the same time I am constantly impressed by meeting people – from all the churches – who struggle sincerely and painfully to live the Gospel. They do not always have an easy time remaining within the church. People who stay, those who leave, and those who cannot bring themselves to cross the threshold, all grapple with the same problem, summed up by an occasional churchgoer for whom the jury is still out: 'To me, the church is like a building with walls of glass. You look through the glass, and sometimes it gives you a vision of God – or at other times it may be that all you see is a distorting mirror. And each time you go, you can't tell which it is going to be.'

Trying it on for size

2

To go or not to go – what draws us to church?

'I'm thinking of joining a church,' said Janet to friends around her dinner table, shortly before her sixtieth birthday. Seeing the bewilderment of her guests, she added, 'Well, sixty is a big milestone. I really am entering on the final phase. So I think I'd better get in there, set the record straight.' Although she herself had not been more than an occasional churchgoer in her adult life, Janet did not question the place of church in society. It existed to preach and to teach, and to focus on the deeper things of life, which to her were intensely private. She had felt – and still felt – no particular need to talk with others about those things, and was a practical person who was somewhat allergic to overt piety. Moreover, she had few illusions about the behaviour of churchgoers. 'I've got two ministers living in the flat above me,' she said, 'and you can guess who puts out the dustbins.' Nevertheless she saw the church as in some way responsible for another level of existence, and – in the form of a sensitive Church of Scotland minister – it had served her well at the time of her mother's death. Now, some years later, she believed that the time had come to place herself within the church community. A few weeks after her birthday she did just that.

We could say that Janet is fortunate in that she has a clear idea of what she believes and of the role the church should play in that. As she embarks on this 'final phase' of her life, it is clear to her that now is the time to enter the fold, to reflect on the church's teaching, and to become an active member of its community – all part of setting her spiritual affairs in order.

There are, however, many different ways of relating to the church, of being 'in' and 'out', and they are not always so clear-cut.

Besides the regular members, there are people who attend from time to time, or who like to mark major events in their lives such as marriage or the birth of a child by a service. Even to someone who rarely goes inside a church building, the presence of the church in the background as part of the fabric of society may be very important. There are those who belong to the church simply by virtue of having been baptised as babies, but never give it a moment's thought. And there are those for whom staying away from church signifies that it has had a powerful effect on them. There is a story of a young soldier signing up to fight in World War Two. Asked his religion, he replied 'Atheist'. 'You can't have that,' said the sergeant, 'you've got to *be* something.' 'But that is what I am,' he replied, and insisted on having his religion recorded in this category, even if they had to make a new one just for him. The young man in question was the son of Geoffrey Fisher, who became Archbishop of Canterbury in 1945.

In some ways, then, church operates like a family: it can be a firm foundation or a source of painful or ambivalent memories and feelings; it may be something we need to shut out altogether, at least for a time. It can also be the family we never had or the family we have lost. It may be a place where we seek relatives of an earlier, more church-oriented generation, trying to discover what was important to them in their lives. And mostly we find that, like a family, the church just goes on being there regardless of our individual feelings.

Whatever the nature of our approach, 'Mother Church' may welcome us with open arms, or leave us feeling outside, unworthy, rejected. She may inspire us with her sanctity, or appal us with her priggishness. She may reveal herself as a hotbed of dirty politics, or as a community of people genuinely struggling to find Christ in each other. She may go whoring after prestige, riches and sentimentality, or she may touch us with her simplicity and awe. She may cover up guilty secrets, or foster honesty and repentance. She can be as accepting as the father of the Prodigal (Luke 15:11ff.), or shut her doors as firmly as that of the bridegroom closed to the foolish virgins (Matthew 25:12).

We, too, of course, can find ourselves reacting differently at different times. Our needs change, our circumstances change, and while in theory the church should be large enough to accommodate whatever goes on in our lives, this is not always the case. Once we have some sort of awareness of church, however, it can be very hard to ignore it altogether. The question 'Do you go to church?' often elicits a guilty or anxious look, and a response such as 'Not as much as I should'; 'Not for some time'; 'It is something I think about sometimes'. One person said, 'I really don't like the church, but whenever I decide to let it go altogether, I just get swamped by guilt.' Someone who was staying away from the church after a particularly bad experience said that it was safest to ignore it as far as possible: 'If I pay attention, I shall realise I need it. I need to protect myself from my own needs.' What an extraordinarily complex statement: in spite of the damage, the need does not go away, and she does not expect to fulfil that need in any other way. So the only thing to do is to avoid being reminded of how powerful that need is.

This person's experience is, however, some way down the line, and our concern in this chapter is what draws people in to the church. In the stories that follow, we will find an interplay between what comes from within and what comes to us through people and events in our lives. From within we find desire for shared mystical experience, a search for meaning, the development of intellectual conviction; and from without we see the influence of family, friends, mentors and writers. We will also see that the factors that bring us into church are not necessarily overtly 'spiritual' at all. Since we are dealing with a very complex institution as well as with the extraordinary variety of human experience it would not make sense to try to pin down the factors that emerge from the stories that follow too narrowly. What we do see, however, is a great variety of expectation and experience.

'My soul has a desire and longing to enter into the courts of the LORD' (Psalm 84:2)

Whether we consciously experience it or not, the desire for God that the Psalmist refers to seems to be in some way built into us as human beings: 'You have made us for yourself and our hearts are restless till they rest in thee,' as St Augustine put it.[1] It is not, of course, something that we necessarily experience as a desire for church as such, but it is one of the things that draws people towards the church. Sometimes we even find there a strong sense of God's presence.

Among those who have not found a spiritual home in the churches few have the logical detachment of the man who said, 'I'm pro-church if it is doing its job of mediating the Spirit. If not, why bother? Two years ago I went to Christmas Eve communion and there was spiritual presence. Last year there was none. It's not really worth worrying about.' As a businessman, he saw the church as having a job to do. If it was doing it that was fine, but if not then it could be dismissed. If only life were always so simple! Many of us find it hard to let go so easily, and those who continue to search may find themselves coming and going, or moving between churches, in a way that 'hard-core' church members find irritating. Yet what is sometimes seen as mere 'spiritual consumerism' is often the result of painful and sincere desire not only for God, but for a community that might make it possible to believe, as is eloquently expressed by one occasional churchgoer: 'I find it difficult to know whether to go to church or not. Sometimes I walk in there, and it is quite obviously God's house. There is an atmosphere of prayer, and the people themselves all seem kind of at one with it and each other. I feel completely at home. Then there are other times, when it is as though I knock at the door and a person appears with a clipboard and says "God? Did you say you were looking for someone called God?" And I say, "Well, he was here – he was definitely here a couple of months ago." And they look down at their clipboard – they might even go to a desk and flip through a book of records – and say "Mmm ... God. No. Sorry. No one of that name here. No, you must be mistaken." '

For this person, the point of going to church is to be drawn into the presence of God. She believes in God, and that God can be found in art, music, loving relationships and so on. By going to church, however, even if only now and then, she is moving beyond a simply personal faith to a shared experience of that faith which draws not only on the presence of the other people there, but on everything that goes to make up the service: the building itself, the images within it, the Christian story as expressed in the liturgical tradition, the hymns, the readings, the prayers – all the things that unite worshippers across time and space. In the experience of one-ness, she feels 'completely at home'. At other times that experience is simply unavailable.

Claire, who had stopped going to church during a very chaotic period in her teens when she felt herself to be beyond the pale, only returned as a regular member some thirty years later. Even so, she said, 'I don't think there was ever a year when I didn't set foot inside a church. I would listen to the music and the hymns – that was quite comforting. It was something I had never really left behind, and I had a sense of exile. I was in a very cold place without it, a desert.'

This sense of exile is shared by a man who is still working out what his relationship with the church is: 'In the midst of all my negativity I have a longing for a part of it – I'm just not sure what that part is.' There is a mystical aspect to this longing which goes beyond the personal. We are created as social beings, and however much each individual's search for God may be a personal matter, the desire to participate in something larger than ourselves is part of it, as described by a church member who, much as she would like to, finds herself unable to dispense with church: 'Mystical truth lies within each person, and the role of the church is to make common what is experienced in a deeply private place.' Alongside the search for a common experience is that for a common faith and understanding that underpins that experience and makes sense of it: 'The most important thing about the church is reverence, ritual, having a vocabulary, having meaning, sacrament,' said one young woman.

Becoming a regular member of a church does not, of course, do away with the longing: rather it can enable it to become part of our lives, and nourish it and allow it to deepen. 'Church is very important to me', said a woman who combined a large family with a job, 'as a place where I do not have to do anything – you just have to *be*. Other people are doing – singing in the choir, serving and so on, but for me, I just want to go there. It is like being held. You just are there, and respond to what goes on.'

The mystical soul tends to respond primarily at this level: if the worship expresses an experiential truth and is spiritually nourishing, the rest can take care of itself. 'I used to do a great deal of reading,' the same woman said, 'and I got tremendously worried because I couldn't get my head around atonement. And then I found no one else could either, so I didn't have to worry. In fact I don't worry about the intellectual side at all any more. I ignore what I can't cope with – such as a great deal of St Paul – and don't let it put me off. Theory is enlightening, but it is always lacking.'

The sense of connection which shared worship provides can, of course, be very seductive, particularly when it is highly ritualised . 'I was drawn to the Orthodox Church', said a convert, 'because of the music, the continuity, the icons, the awe, the stillness, the drama of the liturgy and the sense of seriousness.' Some years later, she still felt that the liturgical worship was the important thing; friendship and theological discussion were valuable by-products; pastoral care had not really featured in her church life – but she continued to be nourished in some undefined way by the sacraments.

Similarly, an Anglican for whom the Eucharist forms the heart of her church experience described it as 'a framework in which things can happen: you come out at the end different from when you went in. I find that if I am not able to go to the Eucharist for some reason, I fret, I really notice. There isn't anything else that can take its place.'

Not everyone finds ritual attractive in itself, however, and it is easy to be put off by something that seems over-prescribed, or that we do not understand. On the other hand, what goes on in churches is many-layered, and our responses can change over time as the rhythm of worship itself draws us in. A young woman who is now a full-time lay pastoral worker in the Anglican Church joined her chapel choir while at university 'only for the music. I wanted to join a choir and the chapel choir was the best one.' For the first term, she 'hated the chapel ritual', having the impression that it was 'everyone doing and not thinking'. Then, she said, 'I got it'. It so happened that her room-mate in college was a Christian, and this helped her enormously in developing her understanding of Christianity: 'I could talk to her about any faith questions, or what had been said in the sermon, or anything I didn't understand.'

From the church we also, of course, seek understanding of what Christians believe, and the implications this might have for our lives. At the very least there is the supportive effect of being among other people who believe the same things and express it in the services: 'You say to yourself, "Well, they are still going, they feel it is important ..." ' But coming together to worship is also about keeping on track, deepening our understanding of the world, our place in it, and our relationship with God.

Turning to the church in crisis – an urgent need for meaning

Another powerful influence that brings people to church is personal crisis – bereavement, illness, anything that makes us question the meaning of our experience. Jane's story is typical: 'I gave up going to church after I left school, because it wasn't interesting. But years later, when my brother-in-law had a bad accident, my sister and I looked around for a church. We found one, and we have gone regularly ever since.'

One woman described how she found her way back in to the church as the result of a love affair coming to an extremely painful end. She herself ended it because she and her husband had a child, and she loved them and could not bring herself to leave them. 'I came back to church because of that relationship,' she said. 'I had to find a way to live without him that could make me see all this in a more truthful light.' By turning to the church she was not seeking escape. Although it was the pain of ending that relationship that brought her to church she was troubled by the attitude she found among some people there, that God inflicts suffering to show people something. 'I do think, however,' she said, 'that suffering itself sometimes shows us a path. I had to give up that relationship, and it was the suffering that showed me I had to do that.' In prayer, she added, 'we will not necessarily get what we want, but we can understand better how to live through experience. Julian of Norwich says, "All will be well" – I believe that, though we don't understand how.'

It is sometimes said that death is the last frontier that secularism has not succeeded in taking over from the church. Death is certainly something that leads us to search for ways of understanding what faith has to say about death, and I have never talked with a bereaved or about-to-be-bereaved person (including myself!) who did not raise questions like: do we really believe in some kind of afterlife? Where? What is it like? Are people punished for what they have done? What do we mean when we say in the creed that we believe in the resurrection of the body? What is judgement? And so on. Faced with the reality of the death of someone we love, like C. S. Lewis in his journal written after his wife's death, we are forced to question what we really think might be going on.[2]

Frances's story (1)

Frances is someone whose story we shall refer to at various points in our exploration. It was a series of bereavements over a short space of time that made Frances desperate to understand what Christians really believed about death. Frances grew up in a churchgoing Anglican family, who sent her to a church-run boarding school. Even as a child she had difficulties reconciling her response to the worship which she loved – she describes the services in the school chapel as 'lovely, sweet memories' – with Christian dogma: 'Odd things would jar on me.' She has particular difficulty with the story of the Fall in Genesis, and the idea that evil came into the world through Eve, through women. 'That myth', she said, 'made me angry even as a child. Everything is taken so literally and there is so much bigotry. Are people thinking about what they are saying?'

At university Frances mixed with people of all faiths and none, including a number of disaffected Catholics who had left the church because of the attitudes to women, and she too left the church: 'It sounds as though I was easily swayed – but it wasn't that. It was that other people made sense.' 'I have to admit,' she said, 'that I didn't try that hard to get answers – I wasn't that interested in church. There had been some lovely moments – it is all part of your life, and I loved it – but then what?' She became an atheist because, she said, 'I came to believe that most Christians needed a crutch. It wasn't belief in God, but wishful thinking, because they could not face reality.' She went on to marry and enjoy a successful career.

Many years later, several close friends died in quick succession, and suddenly the question of whether belief in God was real or not became an urgent issue. Someone suggested Frances visit a local convent, and her initial response was, 'What on earth for?' It struck her as a bizarre idea. One afternoon, however, she simply drove to the convent, knocked on the door and asked to speak to someone. 'What is it about?', asked the nun who opened the door. 'I want to know what you are all doing here,' she replied. The nun looked at her, and then invited her in to talk with one of the sisters. 'I wanted to know what it was they believed – and why,' said Frances, 'or was it all just blind faith? The nun I spoke to was very honest. She acknowledged that they all had difficulty believing at times, so we went on talking.'

It was through this monastic community that Frances found her way in to a church where the liturgy was profoundly nourishing: 'My mystical side found a home in the worship. It was easy to move into it. I was asking and getting answers. It gave me food for thought and took me to a new depth of communion with God. That', she added, 'was before I joined' – and we will return to her story in a later chapter.

I'm only here for the music

Not everyone who walks through a church door is consciously looking for a spiritual dimension. John, a lawyer, began an unexpected journey when he started singing in his chapel choir at university. Like the young woman who began by hating the chapel ritual, he had no religious conviction at the time. 'When I started singing,' he said, 'I was anti-religious on my own account. I had no objection to other people worshipping, but for me it was a chance to sing. It was entirely a musical activity. If anyone had asked me if I believed in God I would have been fiercely anti.' Later, however, he took instruction and was baptised – not so much because of the ritual aspect of the church, but out of intellectual conviction. As part of his university course he had to read the work of John Finnes, a Catholic, on philosophy of law. 'It all coalesced and made sense of how I understood the rest of the world, and the law in particular. It had intellectual and emotional coherence.' He also talked through spiritual questions with friends, and took a great deal of inspiration and spiritual guidance from books. Now, some years after having left university, he still attends his local church with his girlfriend.

Music, which is at the heart of almost all church worship, is a place where mystical longing and shared faith can meet. Through singing hymns together we not only express the story in which we commonly believe but we find ourselves heartened and connected at a deep level that involves our bodies as well as our minds. As the composer James MacMillan points out, music is the most spiritual of the arts: 'One hears of lives being transformed by music, of moods and perspectives being altered, of attitudes shifting, and renewed meaning and purposefulness taking root in lives touched by music.' Even listening to music is, he says, an active process 'analogous to contemplation, meditation and even prayer in the way it demands our time'.[3] Some might even say it is an improvement on what the churches have to offer: a woman who had left the church some years ago lamented the fact that she found the ritual stale and the church stuck in its ways: 'The church should be totally alive to now – like improvising music,' she said.

A man from a non-churchgoing family, now in his thirties, became a churchgoer through playing the organ. He began in his mid-teens, at that time going to church up to four times on a Sunday to play for services. He describes himself as 'a provider rather than a consumer', and it is rare for him to sit in a congregation. In fact, when he does find himself among the congregation, rather than in the organ loft, he usually feels out of place. 'Normally I am one step removed,' he said, 'focusing on the music rather than on the service itself.' He nevertheless gains a great deal spiritually from his part in the service. Like James MacMillan, he believes 'appreciation of music is in its own right a way of getting closer to God'.

For Teresa, also a musician, music brought about a real crisis in her identity as a Roman Catholic. Having been brought up in a staunch Catholic family, she eventually became a specialist in early church music and began to sing in the choir of an Anglican church. After some years she found that she felt 'very much in tune with the Articles of Faith because that is my period of music. There was part of my soul that said, "These people have it right." Though I still thought of myself as a Roman Catholic, I was not going to the Roman Catholic church by choice: I was going to the Anglican church by choice.'

Family, friends and mentors

Our encounters with church – as with all other aspects of our life story – are also profoundly influenced by family background. This can, of course, work in more than one direction: growing up in a church family may instil a lifelong love of the church, or the opposite. Either way, the fact that we *have* grown up with it can make the church in some sense inescapable: we may love it or hate it, but it is built into our identity. Where there is no such background, the church may also be something which we discover and claim as our own as we move away from our families, a place offering new horizons and ways of looking at life.

Margaret has a history and sense of family continuity in the church that is quite unusual now: she grew up attending a church where three generations of her family had worshipped. She was eventually married there, as had been her parents and grandparents, and she values this link with family history, as well as having very happy memories of going to church as a child: 'I used to sit with my grandmother in the front row. My brother was a boat boy, and my father and grandfather were in the choir. My mother went to the eight o'clock service because she had the dinner to cook, but she also taught in the Sunday school.' As a child Margaret found the church building and the ritual and music exotic and beautiful in contrast to the general greyness of the 1950s: 'I loved being there.' She considered it a real privilege when she was deemed old enough to go to the early morning services before people went to work: it was 'a sign of being grown up'.

Although Margaret stopped going to church in her late teens, she began again after her marriage, when she had small children. This was in a different town from her original church, but the local congregation was very welcoming, and she is still an active member of the church thirty years later.

Teresa, who, as we have seen, was seduced by Anglican church music towards the Thirty-Nine Articles, comes from a very traditional Roman Catholic family, with two monastic uncles. She was extremely religious as a child, and wanted to be a nun and a missionary doctor. 'It was both my own ambition and the family's: once the child expresses it, the family tries to foster it.' Although she never did become a nun she still, in late middle age, wonders if she might be a 'missed vocation': 'I am contemplative, but I don't feel called to do that within the structure of any church.' Teresa attended a Catholic school and thrived on the structure of prayer and instruction that went with it: 'Every lesson started and ended with prayer,' she said, 'and we had Mass every day at the seminary across the road. It was very structured. I loved it.' She paid tribute to the education and understanding her Catholic upbringing had given her: these were treasures which she would not wish to be without: 'I still very much believe that way, though I've moved aside from the Catholic Church.' She is, nevertheless, the only one of several adult siblings who still goes to church; one brother went so far as to gain a doctorate in theology and study for the priesthood, but he married, and 'has not set foot in church since'.

'My brother and I were *sent* to church,' said Michael. 'I remember in my childhood realising there was something not quite right about that. There was a feeling that children needed to be indoctrinated into this because it would change their lives, but it didn't seem to find its way through into other people's lives.' He remembered being embarrassed at school because he was a churchgoer, but also experiencing church itself as an organisation like any other: 'Some people were quite nasty and horrible, some were quite nice, and most were both at different times.' At eleven he had confirmation classes, which involved a battle with his mother because she thought he was too young. The classes did not, however, make any great impression, nor did the experience of being confirmed: 'I don't remember any deep feeling of relationship to God or what it was about.' Again, church music, on the other hand, did get through to him, both at the everyday and at the mystical level. It brought 'a sense of recognition' in the community, since he began to play the organ for services. At the same time, he said, 'When I was playing there was something' – and music continues to be the wellspring of his spiritual experience.

As well as family, friends are, of course, an enormous influence in our lives, whether they know it or not. During a critical period in adolescence, Claire found herself floundering in a major depression and the church as such was not able to help her. When she tried to read the New Testament it made matters worse: 'All I could see was the violence, the casting out of those who did not conform. I felt I was cast out.' The presence of a particular friend in the church was crucial. 'I wanted to be part of the church but it was impossible to hold onto it in any way. I think I was quite disapproved of in the church community. I was just too maverick – difficult to deal with, and angry. I didn't take for granted what was said to me. But I didn't want to lose it. For me faith was a beacon of hope. I didn't like the people particularly, and I spent most of my time with non-believers, but I did want the idea of something beyond that could lift me out of my misery.' Although she did 'drift off' from the church for many years, she eventually came back. Throughout she stayed in touch with her friend, whom she thought of as 'very religious, very upright – a decent human being' – and whose existence helped her think well of the church.

It is friends rather than family who are the first contact with church for many adolescents and young people: they go to church 'because my girlfriend likes it' or 'because I got in with a crowd'. One woman described how she started going to church when she moved to London for her first job, and it turned out that her flatmates were all churchgoers: 'The flat, the church and work became my whole world.' Sue, now a Sunday school teacher, started going to church as a child 'because the sweet shop was closed on Sunday, and it got me out of chores'. She now teaches at a Sunday school where none of the children's parents come to church.

As we have seen, some people who start going to church without any particularly spiritual agenda in mind detect a further dimension in what they find there. Beverley, for example, began going to church when she was fourteen because she wanted to go to the youth club with some friends from school. 'If you wanted to go to the youth club then you had to go to church.' There was no other link between the church community and the teenagers – 'no teaching or anything – it was simply a question of ticking the box. I'm not sure that BCP evensong was the best introduction for a 14-year-old,' she added, 'but I have never really left, even though I often wonder what I am doing.'

After her youth club days, Beverley continued going to church because 'I lived with a regular churchgoer and I sang'. During this period she was confirmed, which 'felt special', and began to receive communion, but church remained at the surface of her life. For some years she 'bobbed in and out' and only resumed regular churchgoing after she married and was in the process of settling down, 'because I wanted to hook into the community'. Being a very practical person, she soon found herself taking on various jobs and 'it snowballed'. At this point, Beverley was still relating to church at a primarily social level, but the community changed dramatically when the vicar left, and was replaced by a traditional Anglo-Catholic. It was her first encounter with incense, and with the veneration of Mary. 'He managed to alienate the entire congregation,' she remarked, 'and most people left.' Beverley herself stayed on, again primarily for social reasons, because she believed in the local parish system, and did not want to change churches simply because the way of worshipping had changed. 'Then,' she said, 'I found that this kind of worship gave me a sense of the numinous.'

Beverley's relationship with the worship of the church deepened, and around the time that women were beginning to be ordained in the Church of England, she felt the stirrings of a vocation to the priesthood. Ironically, of course, the very person who had brought her to this point was opposed to the ordination of women. He did, however, support her: 'He generously said he thought I had a vocation even though he could not recognise it.' He put her in touch with the right people, and in due course she became a priest herself.

An important figure in the journey of another woman, who came from a non-church background but was eventually ordained, was her primary school headmistress who took her to Sunday school as a child. She much enjoyed this, and developed a belief in God. In adolescence she stopped going to church, but as a university student she, too, began going to college evensong 'for the music'. Then, during a vacation she visited her ex-headmistress, who asked her what her career plans were. At the time she had no idea, so the headmistress asked her what she wanted from a job. 'When I described the kind of job I would like,' she told me, 'she looked at me very strangely and said, "Why aren't you a priest then?" I can't stress how much that had never occurred to me. I went home and said to my mother, "I want to be a priest," and she said, "Don't be so bloody stupid" – and that was everyone else's response as well.'

The idea might have come to nothing if it had not been for the college chaplain, with whom she talked the following term. Women were only just beginning to be ordained in the Church of England, so the chaplain was a man. When she told him she wanted to be a priest, his reaction was, 'We had better get you confirmed then.' 'One of the reasons I'm a college chaplain now', she remarked, 'is that he had every right to laugh at me and he didn't.'

Not all the people who influence our journeys into the church are personally known to us: a mentor may be a charismatic leader, a writer, a theologian. I was once at a meeting where someone suggested we might study some of Harry Williams's work.[4] There was immediate excitement. 'Yes,' said one person, 'he saved my life when I was an undergraduate.' Another said, 'He converted me to Christianity by his books,' and another, 'I keep his books by my bed in case I wake up in the night and need help.' It was as a result of reading Harry Williams in my early thirties that I myself began to take Christianity seriously for the first time after I had left home. This was because of the extreme honesty with which he approached his autobiography.[5] Here was not only a Christian but a priest who was open about his love for another man, who admitted to psychological fragility and breakdown, who had needed – and benefited from – psychoanalysis. At the time a close friend of mine was dying, and, like Frances whose story we began above, I was much in need of a sense of meaning. I wrote to Harry Williams about it. He not only replied but stayed in close touch throughout the following months. Though we never met, his response and support were – and are – crucial in my relationship to the church.

Celia's story (1)

The influence of particular people – both in person and in books – can be clearly seen in the first episode of a story we shall follow at various points throughout this book, that of a woman whom we shall call Celia, whose relationship with church began with her baptism as a baby in the early 1930s. Celia's parents were atheists but she was baptised 'to please the grandparents'. Her first visit to church was to Harvest Festival at a village church when she was eight: 'We were intrigued by the novelty and by such things as the bunches of grapes surrounding the pulpit. My brother asked if they were there for the vicar to eat during the sermon.' The war years saw a number of moves: 'Local clergy would visit but generally seemed to afford my parents some amusement.'

From this time onwards a number of different influences were at work in Celia's journey towards the church, in spite of opposition from her family. The first was that of the nuns at a convent where she had music lessons: 'I was impressed by the quiet and dignified bearing of the sisters there, but my grandmother affirmed that Roman Catholics were "in league with the devil" and my parents withdrew me.' Celia was a reclusive adolescent, and the words 'church' or 'God' held no meaning for her. Nevertheless, she was intrigued by a series of articles in *The Listener* by Canon Demant.[6] She went on to read *Practice of the Presence of God* by Brother Lawrence:[7] 'I was entranced by it, especially by the notion that we ought to act with God in the greatest simplicity, speaking to him frankly and plainly, and imploring his assistance in our affairs just as they happen.'

At twenty, Celia fell in love for the first time, with a man we shall call Robert. She was by now a music student, and worked as an au pair for a couple in the town where her college was. Both Robert and her music professor read C. S. Lewis, and recommended *The Screwtape Letters* to her.[8] She also sang in the parish choir and began confirmation classes. All this rapidly came to an end, however, as the Sunday services clashed with the time she was most needed for childminding: 'After an exchange of words on the subject I was sent home to my parents.' Celia was, of course, somewhat traumatised by this experience, but Robert came home for the Christmas vacation. They became more closely involved, Celia became pregnant, and her parents hid her away in a country hotel until the baby was born. 'Being pregnant (for me)', said Celia, who went on to have four more children, 'has always had some life-affirming and God-seeking quality about it and I attended the local church there.' Here, perhaps, we see the advantage of a non-church background: someone in her situation who had been brought up within the church – particularly at that time – might well have felt as shut out from church as she was from family.

Meanwhile the couple's parents 'had an unseemly quarrel of Capulet and Monatgu proportions', the couple were separated 'until such time as we could "prove" ourselves', and the baby was placed with a foster-mother while they completed their studies. On graduating, Robert was sent abroad, and that was the end of the relationship. Celia worked in primary schools to support herself and pay for the baby's keep: 'I re-enacted nativity plays with the little ones, but my heart was frozen. I knew the time was running out that would give us [herself and the baby] an opportunity to know each other.'

At twenty-four Celia married a man who accepted her first child into the family, and they went on to have another child. Her mother-in-law was 'a loving and devout Christian in the High Church tradition', and both children were baptised. It was while pregnant with her third child that Celia first really experienced God as meaning anything to her personally. There were complications in the pregnancy, necessitating a very distressing – and isolating – stay in hospital in another town: 'One night the night sister found me awake and upset and sat beside me and talked about God and about the need to have faith. I realised that all the good people in my life had this sort of unquestioning faith (or so it appeared) and I wanted to be like them.'

After the safe birth of this child, Celia began confirmation classes at her mother-in-law's church: 'I had by now become extremely devout, attending the early morning service each day before breakfast and observing all the days of obligation as well as the Sunday Mass we went to as a family.' When she became pregnant again on 25 March (Feast of the Annunciation) it seemed almost like a sign: 'I became devoted to the Blessed Virgin, of whom there is a lovely representation in this particular church.' The priest in charge heard her first confession just before she was confirmed in May, and that evening brought her a bunch of lilies of the valley from the vicarage garden. She felt uplifted in a way she had never felt before. At the moment of confirmation, Celia 'felt truly welcomed by God in the power of the Spirit'. Here we will leave Celia for the time being, but we shall return to her story later.

3

The 'service-provider' and the community: a question of hospitality

As soon as the search for God takes us beyond the privacy of our own hearts into the church, there is another factor involved – other people: the two or three, or two or three hundred, gathered together, and all that they represent in terms of what we are supposed to believe, or how we – or they – might assume we should behave. As we have seen, the influences that bring us through the church door are complex, and this raises questions for church communities about how to welcome people in a sensitive way. It is easy to assume that people who choose to pray and worship together with others necessarily want to be part of a community, yet the relationship between the two is far from simple.

This is one of the great conundrums of church life: we meet together for shared worship, and in the process of that may experience tremendous unity not only with the others present, but with the church at large. At the same time, each one of us in church is alone before God. As one churchgoer put it: 'If you join a choir you are all doing the same thing – but in church, you are *not* all doing the same thing. You don't know what is happening to anyone else, or even what anyone else is there for. I like that because it puts you all on a level.' But what are we to make of it once the service is over? There are people who thrive on the bazaars, the church coffee, the barbecues, and people to whom these are a barely necessary evil. There are those who feel that being part of the same worshipping community carries certain obligations, and others who find this a bizarre idea: 'People come together to worship –

end of story. I never contemplated meeting people or having contact with them outside,' said one young man. 'Faith is a personal matter, and church is the place I go to worship, not to meet people or study.'

Worshipping together: the church as service-provider

As a 'service-provider', the church fulfils a need for people who want to pray but find it difficult to do so alone, as well as for those whose prayer is enhanced by communal worship. It also provides access to the sacraments, and to its own teaching. A desire for these things does not necessarily, however, go with a desire to take part in any kind of social activities with other churchgoers. Meg spent most of her teens heavily involved in her local church. She then had little to do with church for most of her adult life, but started going again in her early sixties. Quite deliberately, however, she chose not to go to one of a number of parish churches within easy reach, but to a cathedral in the centre of town. 'I simply want to be there for services,' she said, 'and I know that if I go to a local church I will get drawn in to all kinds of activities. I've done all that. I don't mind if they smile and say hello, but I don't want to get drawn in.'

Similarly, a man who had moved to London from a town where he had been actively involved with the local church found it refreshing simply to go to evensong on Sunday evenings. 'I felt I should do something, and it was quite OK. It was quiet, anonymous, low key, no pressure. Something my girlfriend and I did together at that time.'

Having myself grown up in a vicarage, with parish life writ large in our home, I have great sympathy with those who have a need simply to go to church and go away again without getting involved in the community. This is not only the case with visitors, but with some regular churchgoers as well. A young man whose father had been very influential in the local Methodist church when he was growing up, abandoned church life when he left home. 'After a while,' he said, 'I found there was something sadly missing, and so of my own free will I decided to go back. The funny thing is that I have a big problem in taking an active part in the church. I don't participate in any groups or take any official positions. In fact once they asked me to take the collection and I panicked. I just couldn't bear it. But I go every Sunday and I feel I need to be there and I want to be there. I look forward to it, and on the odd occasion when I can't be there I get quite upset.'

'I prioritise services,' said another churchgoer, 'they provide a clear space for me to think.' The majority of her friendships were outside the church community, and the social aspect of church was marginal from her own point of view. 'I try to do my bit,' she said, 'but that's all – and I am no good at organising church events. Some people adore it, but I remember my mother couldn't bear it and used to hide when there was anything like that going on.'

How do we relate praying together with a group of people, and even experiencing ourselves as deeply at one with them during that time, when we may have very little in common with them in ordinary life? 'For me,' said Michael, 'being in church is part of a struggle between a longing to be together with others and a longing to be alone. What I really find difficult is to separate myself from other people in church – and actually that is ridiculous because really belonging to church is about belonging to people – yet I don't even want to know the people around me.' Yet, if we experience one-ness in shared worship, should we not, at the very least, be able to get on with each other over coffee afterwards? And if that one-ness extends beyond the immediate congregation to the world at large, how should this be expressed?

The church community

In any encounter with church, the general attitude of the church community, of course, affects the way we feel. 'We had a good parish priest and a lot of good people,' said one man about the church where he grew up. 'We mucked in with the bellringing, jumble sales and so on – there were good folk around, and it was a normal part of life.' He had also sung in the church choir from the age of ten, and, like so many others, gained a great deal spiritually from singing works like the Bach and Schutz *Passion*s and *The Messiah* in county music festivals.

For some people, it is the social aspect of the church as community, and in the community, that really makes it worthwhile. 'I would always hope and expect to plug in to the local community,' said one woman. 'The best thing about church for me is the sense of fulfilment through helping and being friendly.' Another described her church community as 'a kind of ongoing family. Members come and go but the family carries on. I like it when we have events. There is so much richness in people's lives, and everyone there has a story.' The church community brings together acquaintances, rather than close friends, and this is valuable to her: 'You might only chat two or three times a year, but you do it every year.'

'I kept going to church all through my marriage break-up,' said another. 'It was a time of chaos in my life, and it was so important that there was that structure: the same group of people would be there week by week.' Ann, who had attended church for some years and also found herself in the midst of a divorce, had the opposite experience. She was horrified to find, when her marriage broke up, that people stopped speaking to her, and she stopped going. 'It doesn't mean I don't believe in God,' she said, 'I do, but I don't see what church has to do with it. Church is a community activity. What interests me in a church is what happens after the service. Is there coffee? Do people get to know each other? Are people friendly?'

Feeling at home

Feeling at home – whether spiritually, culturally or in some other sense – is important to churchgoers, and culture plays a large part in this. 'I like ceremony and ritual,' said a man who had been baptised into the Anglican Church as an adult, 'but I would not want to tie my spirituality to Anglicanism. I am an Anglican but that is just a matter of culture. It is the world I have been brought up in.'

James grew up in the Anglican church at home and at boarding school, and continued to attend chapel at university. He took church seriously – so seriously that at one stage he considered putting himself forward for ordination, and he so much wanted to understand Christian theology that he took a further degree in the subject. This had an unexpected outcome: the critical study of biblical texts so undermined his beliefs that he subsequently had nothing to do with church for some time. Nevertheless, there was a period shortly after the birth of his first child when he and his family lived in a village in the English countryside. By this time James had studied a number of spiritual traditions, but he decided at this point to go back to church, drawn by the familiar cultural roots: 'I liked the idea of the club,' he said, 'the walk to church with the baby in a rucksack on my back, the 1662 Prayer Book, the beautiful old church, the pub on the way home ... it was an attractive ritual, and I enjoyed it: the architecture, the music, the words ...'

A search for home can, of course, be driven by trying to get away from one's roots as much as by the desire to rediscover them. This can be a risky process, since embracing a spiritual tradition that is not rooted in one's own culture is open to the possibility of doing so in an unrealistic way, that idealises it and does not attempt to integrate it with ordinary life. This is a potential problem for Western converts to Eastern religions in general and the Orthodox Church in particular, since its cultural roots are very different from our own. At an ecumenical meditation group last year I was asked – as the only Orthodox present – what it meant to be Orthodox, and I found this a very difficult question. People tried to help out. 'They have very long services,' volunteered one person, and another said, 'People come and go as they please.' These comments, though accurate, did not seem to get to the heart of the matter. Then the leader of the group asked what we believed. I tried to explain that as Orthodox we believed the same things as other Christians, but attempted to get back to the early roots of the church, taking our traditions – and indeed our liturgy – from the early centuries of Christianity. 'So you mean it is a kind of Christian Sufism?', she asked. I felt I had radically misrepresented Orthodoxy, but in such a positive light that I could not bring myself to disagree, and went away thinking, 'If only ...'.

As a child of the vicarage, highly ambivalent towards church in any form, I was drawn to Orthodoxy in the late 1980s by a sense of spiritual homecoming in the liturgy. At the same time the fact that no one was quite at home in my local Orthodox church was deeply attractive, since it allowed me to be both at home and not at home at the same time. Everyone in that community was in a real sense a stranger, being either 'foreign' – mainly Russian or Greek (even if they had been settled in this country for decades) – or, if they were British, converts to Orthodoxy.

One thing, then, that made it a very lively community was that everyone was, as it were, in exile, and a consequence of that was that everyone needed to be hospitable to everyone else – the British converts because it was our country, and the cradle Orthodox because it was their church. Furthermore, the community as a whole was neither 'Russian Orthodox' nor 'Greek Orthodox' but 'Orthodox'. There were two parishes, one of which was in the jurisdiction of the Moscow Patriarchate and the other within the Ecumenical Patriarchate, but they formed one community and shared one church, with most people going to all the services regardless of who was in charge, this also making it difficult for anyone to feel too much at home or establish any kind of ethnic base – English or otherwise. It also meant that members of the church community had deep and important connections to different local communities outside it, the church forming an unseen link between these. For many years it worked: the focus was on our liturgical life, and it provided spiritual nourishment and social support for a great many people at all kinds of levels. Celebrating the liturgy together, observing one tradition, even if we used several different languages and styles of singing, was a powerful experience of transcending cultural difference.

Such a system is extremely fragile, and heavily dependent on conditions in a particular place. It also requires an immense amount of maintenance – in our own case we not only had three different choirs to cope with different musical traditions and languages, but two parish councils, and a joint parish council who worked hard at maintaining balance in the services and in the community. One of the strengths of our situation was that the branch of the church to which we belonged had begun in exile, founded by the first wave of émigrés after the Russian revolution only a few decades before. Our founders, some of whom were still alive and in church with us, had experienced first hand, and in practice, that 'there is no abiding city'. This concrete experience of exile no doubt spoke to the sense of spiritual exile experienced by many of us who joined them. They had something very precious to offer us in the spiritual tradition they brought with them, but it had had to take root where it found itself.

Today, the situation is very different, not only for us but for all the worldwide churches. In an age where there are massive population movements around the world, the relationship of church to culture is problematic for people who understandably want to worship in their own language and with their own traditions. We have seen the effects in this country recently in both the Roman Catholic and Orthodox Churches. Cultural difference also goes much deeper than language or liturgical tradition: it involves fundamental differences in understanding when it comes to questions such as the role of women or sexual mores, and these issues, of course, are tearing apart the Anglican Communion as I write. These large questions are not our concern here, but the important point is that, at the level of individual experience, religion and culture are closely bound up together, and this has a profound effect on whether we find what we are seeking in the churches – or indeed are able to remain in the place where we find spiritual nourishment.

A question of hospitality

It is very hard for churches to get the balance right between welcoming visitors and overwhelming them. I was put off going into churches for years by someone who walked up to me and asked me where I normally worshipped. Since the answer at the time was 'Nowhere' I felt got at and fled. On the other hand, I recently attended a service where at the end the priest stood by the door and greeted everyone with the words, 'God bless you'. 'You, too,' I replied, feeling rather miffed. He had already blessed us – all of us – at the end of the service. Surely now was the time to say hello?

Where worship is highly ritualised, as in my own church, there are strong codes of behaviour, or even dress. Newcomers may assume (often wrongly) that everyone else understands these, and be afraid of getting them wrong – and, of course, be deeply upset if they are told that they have! On more than one occasion I have been asked to meet beforehand with someone coming to my church for the first time and go in with them, so that they would not have to walk through the door alone. It is a request that arouses my sympathy since I found my own first visit there overwhelmingly strange, and when I was received into the Orthodox Church after some eighteen months of attendance and instruction, I wrote a 'welcome leaflet' explaining to newcomers what kinds of things went on in the church, what they could do – and not do – and so on. The intention was to be encouraging to newcomers, but I may have overdone it: a friend looked over my shoulder while I was writing it, and her comment was, 'You mean you went into this place all on your own?'

In some ways, however, ritual provides a better cloak for a visitor than less formal services, since there is plenty to look at other than the people round about. A woman who accompanied her boyfriend to his church, where the service was a so-called 'hymn sandwich' with readings, hymns and preaching, became very agitated during the service: 'They are looking at me as though I don't belong,' she said to her boyfriend, who was a regular member of the congregation. 'No,' he said, 'you are making it up.' Afterwards he decided to check this out with people in the church, and reported back, 'Actually you were right,' he told her. 'They were looking at you and thinking, "Are you a Christian?" You were absolutely right.'

Whatever the style of worship, it can be reassuring to find – as I did myself when I began to go to church again in mid-life – a hidden place to be, in a side chapel, say, or behind a pillar. Having for many years done my best to forget the church existed, I first experienced its hospitality at a contemplative Anglican convent, where for some years I attended the Eucharist, and occasionally stayed in the guest house. These people were dedicated to prayer, their other activities being the guest house, a small printing works and a large garden. The chapel was L-shaped, and guests sat in the arm of the 'L' from which the main chapel was invisible, yet whenever one was in there, one knew that someone was in the main chapel praying silently. I spent many hours in the guest part of that chapel. The only time I saw the main chapel was at communion, when we came forward to join the sisters around the altar. I came to know them in a deep way, although I rarely spoke with any of them. For someone who found any hint of 'parish life' all but unbearable, this was an exquisitely sensitive welcome.

One of the most well-known Orthodox icons is the icon of the Trinity by Andrei Rublev. This icon is also known as 'The Hospitality of Abraham', and I was first introduced to it by a friend, who said that her therapist kept a copy of the icon in her room. For my friend, it was an image of God's hospitality. 'There are three angels sitting at a table,' she said, 'but the fourth place, the one towards you, is empty. They are making room for you to come in.'

The passage in Genesis 18 which describes the events shown in the icon is one of the most mysterious in the Bible. By the oaks of Mamre, Abraham sees the Lord. He sees three men. Throughout the story the narrative oscillates between these two descriptions of the visitors, and no explanation is given: it is as though we are somehow expected to take it on board as something completely natural. In Rublev's icon we see only the angels, but there are other versions in which Abraham and Sarah are also shown. It is an image from daily life: there is food and drink on the table, and utensils with which to eat it; Abraham and Sarah are placing very ordinary bowls of food on the table. They stand between the angels so that there are two structures that present themselves in much the same way as the two strands of narrative do in the story. There is the circle of perfect communion between the three seated angels; and at the same time there are the two human beings standing attentively, offering them food from behind where they are sitting. Taking a wider view we see: angel – Abraham – angel – Sarah – angel. The two human beings, male and female, offering their own form of hospitality, are brought into communion with the Godhead. It is a liturgical image: 'Thine own, of thine own, we offer thee.' The hospitality is mutual.

Is it possible for the churches to practise hospitality in such a way that people feel welcome, as my friend felt welcomed by her therapist's icon? This is something often discussed at parish meetings all over the world, and it is important. The answers are not always obvious.

Certainly, many people like to be welcomed, to have an interest taken in them, but this interest must be in them as people, not as potential converts, not making the assumption that because someone has crossed the threshold of a church they are ready, or ever will be ready, to be drawn in. It can be even more problematic when a person becomes more sure of their commitment. So often I have seen a new church member given endless jobs to do, because they are new blood, because they will get to know people that way, and so on. And before long, their new relationship with God through the church gets overwhelmed by their encounters with the all-too-human congregation. They become disillusioned and even leave, because they have not been given time to grow spiritually.

There are, perhaps, three different kinds of hospitality. There is generosity which overflows from a sense of abundance – the generosity of God himself in creating the universe. This is easy to give when we are feeling good, but by the same token, it is unlikely to be consistent among human beings, not just because our sense of well-being changes from day to day, but also because as we become involved with people we may find them more difficult than we had previously realised. Then there is the hospitality born of poverty of spirit: when our own suffering teaches us greater compassion for the suffering of others, and we learn to share in the spirit of Christ who emptied himself on the cross. And third, perhaps, there is the hospitality which is built into our shared humanity, which welcomes the stranger for no other reason than that this is what is required – even if the strangers happen to be angels. Someone has travelled to where we are – they must be hungry, thirsty, in need of hospitality, so, like Abraham and Sarah, we bake bread and kill the calf. In our own society, such hunger and thirst may be as much psychological and spiritual as physical, but our human duty is no less pressing.

This opportunity is one which is open to church communities wherever they are, because we are all strangers in a strange land. We live, as we are often told, in a 'post-Christian' society where the ways and attitudes of church are far from mainstream, and church members are swimming against the tide. The education system is deeply wary of any kind of religious instruction which is based on conviction, and much of the Christian tradition has been eroded there. Younger people growing up in ignorance of their own spiritual tradition do not even have the choice whether to accept or reject it. This also, however, has the advantage of shaking us out of mistaking the religious life as any kind of excuse for complacency. It is perhaps from a position of weakness that we have the best chance of sharing the riches of our tradition in a spirit of true hospitality – one which assumes nothing, and knows it must share, not only because we are all – however materially rich – impoverished, but also because God's abundance is sufficient.

This seemed to me to be enshrined in the way a university chaplain described what she observed among the students in her college chapel. She said that she saw newcomers met by 'a real generosity motivated by faith, which says, "You may be isolated, and this may not be your cup of tea – and you don't have to stand up and say you believe all this – but you are welcome anyway." '

How is the church behaving in people's lives?

4

Witnesses for the defence

The nature of our trial

To be tried by external authorities is a terrifying and horrible thing. We see just how terrifying and horrible it is in the trial of Christ in the gospels: the betrayals, the scheming behind closed doors, the easy incitement of the mob – and its fickleness – the corrupt nature of the authorities (Pilate covering his own back; Herod not interested in the case, just eager to see Jesus perform a miracle (Luke 23:8)), and the way the real issues get lost in agendas which have nothing to do with the case. We also see how Pilate himself – the person who holds the key to whether Jesus the man will live or die – has no real idea of what is going on. This is often the case in trials: the person who ends up being in the seat of judgement is usually far removed from the things that matter to the person in the dock. The power of Jesus, and Jesus' whole self-understanding, lies altogether in some other place than the praetorium, as he himself points out: 'You would have no power over me unless it had been given to you from above' (John 19:11).

In this sense, the external trial – though it may destroy us, just as Christ was tortured and killed – is in itself uninteresting. What ultimately counts is the *internal* trial, the point at which any one of us, in whatever circumstances, questions our own integrity, and finds it has or has not survived whatever has occurred. As church, too, as the Body of Christ, this is what ultimately matters. Certainly we should listen to what outsiders have to say, not least because we should want them to see something worth having in the life of the church – but only from within can we really question how we are functioning as the Body of Christ.

Long before Christ is handed over to Pilate, we see this internal level of trial taking place in the gospels. The people who dropped everything to follow him soon find that, whatever the original attraction, the message is hard to assimilate. This is hardly surprising, since two thousand years later we still find it hard to take in just what Christ is saying to us, and constantly distort it. One of the greatest gifts given to us by the writers of the gospels is the way they chart these difficulties even among those closest to Christ. There is no pretence that the Apostles come ready-made: they are on a journey of discovery. They may recognise that Jesus is 'the real thing', but like any of us struggling to be church they frequently miss the point, and make the same kind of mistakes as we make today. Often they cannot understand the parables, and need them explained. James and John want to make sure they have the best seats in the Kingdom (Mark 10:35–45). Peter cannot bear the fact that Christ is placing himself in danger (Matthew 16:22). John and the others try to exclude a man who is clearly in touch with God's healing power: 'Teacher, we saw a man casting out demons in your name and we forbade him, because he was not following us' (Mark 9:38). Like the rest of us, they find that following Christ is a steep learning curve. In a sense you could say they are 'on trial' – will they manage to assimilate what Christ is showing them? – but in another sense, Christ himself is 'on trial' throughout the gospels. These people have given up everything to follow him; yet, is he really the Messiah? Is his preaching really transformative? Marvellous though he is, is he just another prophet? Can he really show us God?

Nowhere do these questions arise more painfully than with John the Baptist. John, the final prophet, 'the voice of the Word, the candlestick of the Light, the morning star and Forerunner of the Sun',[1] dedicated for this purpose from conception, who recognised the incarnation while still in the womb (Luke 1:41), who prepared the way, and baptised Christ in the Jordan: even John at one point begins to wonder. He sends two of his disciples to Jesus, to ask, 'Are you he who is to come, or shall we look for another?' And Jesus answers, 'Go and tell John what you hear and see: the blind receive their sight, the lame walk, the lepers are cleansed, the deaf hear, the dead are raised and the poor have good news brought to them. And blessed is anyone who takes no offence at me' (Matthew 11:4–6).

Our witnesses for the defence, then, show us these things happening through the effect of the church on people's lives. Not only have they tried the church on and found that it fits: it has stood up to trial over time, and brought about positive change. Again, our focus is personal experience within church communities: we are not here concerned with the church charities and organisations working – and making a difference – in the world at large, but with individuals within the churches. At the very least, 'Church provides a God-space', as one person put it. 'I don't give much time to God during the week, so church is a time to say "Hey – here I am".' In the stories that follow, we see some ways in which, by saying 'Here I am' – as Samuel said when God called him from sleep – we can find ourselves changed.[2]

A living story of redemption

We have heard how John began going to his college chapel for the music and then discovered the 'intellectual and emotional coherence' of the Christian faith, as a result of which he was baptised. John began from a very private faith. By placing himself within the church, however, he not only showed intellectual conviction, but allowed that conviction to come alive in his own life: 'Becoming a Christian helped me find a sense of forgiveness.' 'Forgiveness is built into the Christian story itself: Jesus accepts all the consequences of sin and lives through them on our behalf. He overcomes, and helps us overcome.' His experience of church has been that it, too, was living out this story. 'The way Christ overcomes is found actively in the church,' he said, 'in the way people are Christ-like. I was made welcome without reservation. This was something new – and practical as well as theoretical.' As time has gone on, he has found that there is 'something reliable about the Christian context'. He has been repeatedly impressed by a 'generous attitude' in churches and Christian organisations. Even when there have been disagreements, his experience is that both he and the other person would always at least attempt to be friendly because of the shared framework of belief.

This story of redemption is, of course, embedded in the Eucharist, which reminds us of God's total self-giving in Christ, but it is also something we take part in here and now. 'The Eucharist provides a space for forgiveness,' said Claire, an Anglican. 'There is a complete fit between that and my life. The longer I am in the Church the more aware I am of how much better I could be doing as a person.' Her comment is reminiscent of the prayer in the Orthodox liturgy immediately after the invocation of the Holy Spirit on the bread and wine: '*That for those who partake they [the gifts of bread and wine] may be for vigilance of soul, remission of sins, communion of thy Holy Spirit, fulfilment of the kingdom of heaven, freedom to speak in thy presence, and not for judgement or condemnation.*' In other words, sharing in communion is not only finding ourselves loved and accepted, but about being moved on in some way. Claire's comment on her experience of the Eucharist relates directly to 'vigilance of soul'. Though she did not use that phrase, she went on to expand the idea, since she had found it very hard to explain to non-churchgoers. It is a consciousness of being aware of one's own shortcomings in the presence of Christ's love, and is very hard to explain to people who do not have that experience, who are inclined to see it as a form of self-dislike or even masochism. 'A friend thought I was being too hard on myself,' said Claire, 'but it is not in the sense of "what a dreadful person I am", but just being constantly aware I could do things better. Communion is an acting out of forgiveness as well as being symbolic.'

Where the church manages to witness to both the reality of sin and the reality of love – as experienced by both John and Claire – and invites us in to the story, there is great potential for inner healing, if we can hear and receive that invitation, rather than experience ourselves as cast out or unworthy. In Christ's healing encounters we do not see him denying the reality of sin: 'Go and sin no more,' he says to the woman whom he has saved from stoning for adultery in John 7, and to the others, 'Let him who is without sin cast the first stone.' But at no point does he withdraw the invitation to enter into his presence, to experience ourselves as loved. 'Identifying as a Christian does affect the way I behave,' said a woman who had stayed away from church for many years after breaking down in her teens. 'I was very wild, promiscuous, into my own needs, but there came a point where I could not hide or pretend any more.' Her return to the church in mid-life had not only been a healing experience through the sacraments but also by seeing the Christian story lived out in the local community and by practical actions of church leaders such as Archbishop John Sentamu in the wider world.

Attempting to live the Gospel

Where a church community makes a conscious effort to live the gospel story, it can provide a space where it is possible to share problems, even if we cannot immediately do anything about them. A woman who was desperately trying to gain control of a difficult life, and becoming very angry in the process, found that being in church helped her face the reality of her situation. She was trying to do the right thing, and also full of grief that she might have got it wrong. 'It's no good telling me God looks after everything,' she said, 'and it is no good telling me only I matter.' She was not prepared simply to walk away from it, and for her the church provided support in being a place where the synergy between divine and human action was expressed. God would not provide any quick fixes, but there was at least a possibility of entering into the process of getting at the truth of her situation and doing something about it with God's help.

Similarly, in a family service where the children were asked to describe both happy and sad memories, a little boy put his hand up, and said, 'I worry that my Mummy and Daddy are going to split up.' Someone who was at the service said it was for her the best experience she had ever had of church: 'He clearly felt so safe and supported in that place that he could say that.'

Attempting to live the Gospel will not, of course, do away with conflict within the community, any more than being in the presence of Christ prevented the disciples from quarrelling among themselves. If we know, however, that those around us are making an honest effort to learn and to understand, it can have a powerful effect on our own ability to do so. As one parish priest put it, 'There are rare occasions when justice prevails.' Her parish was in the habit of giving its harvest goods to a shelter for the homeless several miles away, and she suggested they might consider giving them instead to a women's refuge close by. At first there was resistance on the grounds that to be a battered wife was 'not very nice'. Eventually, however, the proposal was adopted – 'And now', she said, 'it is as though it has gone on for ever.'

Even where the subject matter is trivial the learning curve, if well handled, can be quite steep. For example, when I was received into the Orthodox Church in the early 1990s I was shocked to discover that apparently ordinary British citizens in the late twentieth century could think there was any problem with the fact that I wore trousers to church. It first came to my attention when I attended a liturgy in a large Serbian church. As I went in, an English woman who was with me said, 'Don't be upset if the priest doesn't want to give you communion, because you are wearing trousers.' This was a little disturbing, but easily understandable, since this was a church with a strong ethnic culture, different from my own. What was shocking was to discover that there were people in my home community who thought this was an issue worth worrying about, and it was not a question of age or ethnic origin – there were people of all ages and ethnicities among those who did care and among those who did not.

Ten years later the problem had more or less disappeared altogether, but what was helpful to me at the time was the way in which people were prepared to discuss it openly. There were several discussions about dress in church, and I was able to understand that not-wearing-trousers was not so much about wanting to keep women in skirts as the idea that the Sunday liturgy, in particular, was considered a very special celebration. Putting on one's best clothes was not in order to make oneself acceptable, but because every Sunday was a celebration of the resurrection – the old idea of 'Sunday best', in fact. There were people (men!) in the congregation who thought women 'should not strut around in trousers', but this was far from being a mainstream view. A woman who said she found it hard to pray if the female singers in the choir (who in our church are highly visible) were wearing trousers was asked to think about what she was doing in church rather than what other people were wearing, while the singers were asked to think about dressing in ways that did not draw attention to themselves. All this inevitably aroused powerful emotions, but these were eventually diffused by an elderly Russian woman, one of the founders of the parish and someone whose views were highly respected, who simply said, 'The only important thing is that you come to church as yourself' – an important, and often overlooked idea: it is hard to find healing in a situation where one is pretending to be someone else.

Giving shape to our lives: story expressed in the liturgical cycle

Another way in which the church expresses the gospel story is in the liturgical cycle, which speaks to us of the rhythm of life, death and resurrection. In the West the church year begins with Advent, and preparation for the incarnation, culminating in the coming of the Spirit at Pentecost. Although the Eastern and Western Churches celebrate the same major feasts, in the East, the church year begins on 1 September, after the harvest is gathered in. The falling asleep, or 'assumption', of Mary (15 August) is the last major feast of the year, and brings the cycle to an end. Then, in September, the new year begins with the birth of Mary, and this can be seen as a reflection of the life cycle of the earth itself. In her assumption, all is fulfilled and gathered in. She is born as we go down into the darkness of winter, a sign the good seed in the ground will come to fulfilment in Christ. Either way, the incarnation shines as a light in the darkness in the depths of winter, and the resurrection, of course, takes place in the spring, the time of new life.

This pattern is embedded in the hearts of many people who no longer go to church. As as one man remarked, 'The calendar year of the church is so integrated into my whole being that I can't help getting lit up by Christmas and what the story is. It is an amazing story.' The liturgical cycle, as part of the fabric of society, can also provide a secure framework. 'Life for many children is chaotic and unpredictable,' said an Anglican priest. 'Liturgical markers give some sense of stability and continuity, especially in church schools, where at least most of the children know, for example, when it is Advent, and that that is when we prepare for Jesus being born.' Much of the time this works in an almost subliminal way. Recently I went to an Advent carol service at my local Anglican church. Seeing the hymn numbers on the board I was suddenly aware how much, as a child, I had been pleased and excited by the way the hymn numbers went back to the beginning of the book (*The English Hymnal*) when Advent began. It always symbolised a new beginning, as well as the approach of Christmas.

Fifty years ago, of course, the cycle was far more deeply embedded in society, and churches would suddenly fill at Christmas and Easter with the so-called 'duty' visitors. 'It used to be a real jolt', said a man who had grown up in a provincial church in the 1950s, 'to see two hundred people in church when there were usually twenty-five.' This happens less, of course, today, but there are still the 'Christmas and Easter' churchgoers. For those who plug on being the 'two or three gathered together' throughout the year, it can be a wonderful experience to be surrounded by crowds of people celebrating Christ's birth or resurrection – a reminder that the Christian story has relevance beyond the immediate church community.

Likewise, the celebrations of these feasts have an effect beyond those immediately involved. A man who had long stopped going to church was on holiday in Paris with his children one Palm Sunday. They were walking past Notre Dame, just as the bishop was approaching, and there was a huge crowd outside the west door. As part of the ceremony, the bishop approached with his staff and hit the door with it. The door opened, there was a great swell of organ music from inside, and the people thronged into the church carrying their palms. 'It was absolutely overwhelming,' he said. 'Thinking about it still sends shivers down my spine. An experience like that does remind me of the huge importance of the church. There is meaning and structure at the heart of church life for individuals and for the community. However misguided the churches may be, the fact that they go on praying and acting out the Christian story has to be good. There is love at the centre of the story, and we sure as anything notice when it is not there.'

'I will go into the house of the Lord': the importance of place

A man described how, when he was going through a very difficult time as a student, the existence of the college chapel provided him with stability. Although not a particularly ardent believer, he was an organ scholar and had a room near the chapel: 'I often went in there – it was a kind of extension of my home space – and the services were very happy occasions. The chapel was one of the things that kept me going because of the community and the cycle of services.' For him, there had not been any particular personal support or connection in the chapel. What mattered was the building itself and being together with others in services, along with the structure of the liturgical cycle. As far as he was concerned this all took place more or less in spite of the college chaplain – 'a nice guy, but singularly inappropriate and unhelpful' – and he could barely remember the other people who used to come to services: but the coming together and sense of shared purpose remained a good and nourishing memory.

It is not only places in which we ourselves have prayed that can become significant, but places which in general are prayed in. Chapels within institutions like hospitals and colleges can have a profound effect on people's understanding of the whole place, even if they do not often visit them. A man who was involved in the rebuilding of a hospital chapel said he was flooded with letters from people who never used it but for whom its existence was hugely significant: they said that without it the heart of the hospital would be gone.

It is a common experience that a place that is prayed in over time develops a certain atmosphere, and the sense of spiritual depth which many people long for can be more accessible in an empty church building than in shared worship. People who visit churches outside service times are often in a receptive frame of mind. They are looking for something which ordinary life – or indeed other people – cannot give them, and are likewise often very sensitive to what they find there. A picture, a smell, a lamp burning can take on great significance. In the days when I never went to church for services, I would often visit empty churches for the atmosphere, and the sense of a place that had been prayed in. The fact that so few churches are able to stay open for casual visitors is much lamented, and is something that needs addressing where possible. As one person said, 'People need church buildings, even if they are agnostic; they need a place where they can go and pray and possibly talk to someone.'

In recent years the French have done marvellous work in this regard. Many of their country churches are able to remain open; discreet notices welcome visitors and provide suggestions as to how to enter into the silence there in a prayerful way. Sacré-Coeur de Montmartre in Paris has ceased to be the jumble of noise and bustle that it was in the 1970s. Signs all around the church remind visitors that it is a place of prayer, and although there are still many tourists, there is a powerful silence in there.

The great cathedrals that need to charge tourists in order to maintain the building face a huge problem. Even if the contribution is declared to be voluntary, it is not easy to run the gauntlet – as I have done – of the people on hand to take the money, and it all militates against being able to use the cathedrals simply as holy places. Yet they continue to speak to us of the story in which we live.

In Barcelona there is a cathedral that has been under construction for a hundred years: Sagrada Familia, the Holy Family. In the Middle Ages, unfinished cathedrals cannot have been so unusual, but in modern times there is something awe-inspiring about a project that has gone on for so long. It was begun by Antoni Gaudi in 1882, and he worked on it until his death in 1926. It is not expected to be finished until 2026. The east face of the cathedral is a mass of Gaudi's strange, melting iconography, while the western façade is covered with the austere planes depicting Calvary; Veronica, the woman who wiped the face of Christ and found the image of his face on her cloth, is the central figure. This façade, begun in 1987, more than a hundred years after work on the cathedral began, is the work of Josep Maria Subirachs. The older, east face of the cathedral tells the stories of the Bible, Old Testament and New. My daughter – not a churchgoer – who had been entranced by the art and the architecture on a previous visit, took me to Barcelona and particularly insisted I should see Sagrada Familia. As I commented on the various images and their content, she turned to me and said, 'You know, Mum, it is great to be here with someone who knows all the stories.'

As we walked around the inside of the building with its masses of scaffolding, I tried to imagine how it would be when it was finished. It was full of people wandering around with intense interest in the architecture and the images they found there. In its unfinished state it was an extraordinary witness to the Judaeo-Christian story, and I found myself wondering if a functioning cathedral would ever achieve as much.

Communion of saints

The church does not of course exist only in buildings or even in services or good works, but in connections over space and time, which may not be explicit but can be experienced at a deep level, as described by Claire: 'At critical times I continued to pray without any clear sense of what I was doing. When I look back, it seems to me that however desperate I was I was held in some way – through love, through friends. I didn't plummet to the depths. I was given grace, which has enabled me to continue.'

Again Teresa, who as we have seen had a very thorough Catholic education, reached a point in mid-life where she had a crisis of faith, a 'dark night of the soul'. She was sustained in this by a spiritual adviser who reminded her that 'When you can't pray, others are praying for you. '

These connections can be both horizontal, spreading out across the world in our present age, and vertical, existing through time. They can involve people we know, and people we have never met. I have a friend who, after years of battling with insomnia, has now decided to stop fighting it. Instead, she prays most nights between midnight and three a.m. During the months when I was caring for my husband who was dying from cancer, and was often awake at those times, knowing that she was there praying, even if she was not specifically praying for us, was very important to me. On a much larger scale, a Roman Catholic priest described how his sense of connection with the worldwide church came home to him when a priest was murdered in Pakistan: 'I had an immediate sense that these were my brother priests who were being killed.'

If we move beyond the boundaries of our own age, we find connections that transcend time as well as space. By taking part in the services of the church we become part of traditions that go right back to the very beginning, even if they have changed and adapted to our current age, and this connects us with the prayer of people throughout all those generations. Particular figures, or saints in the history of the church or in scripture, can also take on a real personal significance. At the very least, being given the name of a saint can lead you to reflect on the saint's life, and how it relates to your own circumstances. For many people, however, it goes much further than that: just as we can find the church at work in our lives, so it can seem that a particular saint is not just remembered but active in what is going on.

A little-known saint, Melangell, has a shrine just over the Welsh border on the site of a nunnery she founded in the seventh century. It is not only a beautiful church in beautiful surroundings but the atmosphere of prayer within it is almost palpable. Through the work of an Anglican priest – the widow of another priest who loved the place and was for a short time its guardian before he died – it has become a centre for anyone suffering from or working with cancer, as professional or carer. The work goes on both on a practical level and through prayer. When I first visited the shrine, I told my brother about it and about Melangell, and although he was not conventionally religious, it was as though he immediately developed an inward connection with her. We never visited the shrine together as we had planned because he developed a brain tumour shortly afterwards, but the connection remained – not only as a source of strength for him, but in that the people at the shrine prayed for him throughout his illness. Stories like this abound, and although it is easy to dismiss them as pious hope, for those who experience this kind of connection in their hearts, its reality cannot be denied.

A friend in need

Not all the church's activity, of course, takes place among its regular members. 'One thing the church does well', said a non-churchgoer, 'is going on being – being bigger than the individual and a focus for the community.' Although he had long ceased to be an active member, the fact that the church 'as an ongoing thing' had continued to be there throughout a very difficult period in his life had been very valuable to him. For a while, he went to services in a cathedral, which sustained him. 'It helps you remember you are part of something much bigger – it reminded me that what was happening was not the end of my world. It helps you know that you are part of something more.'

Mark described a time when he was under enormous personal pressure at work. False accusations had been made against him, and it was extremely distressing and painful. Although he was no longer an active member of a church he found himself going into the local Anglican cathedral where the Eucharist was just beginning in a side chapel, and stayed for the service. 'I was overwhelmed', he said, 'by finding myself completely accepted and loved by something. I don't know how it happens. It is just amazing and mysterious.' The priest who celebrated that Eucharist and the people who attended it will have had no conscious connection with Mark, and yet being with them in that service was for him a life-changing experience. This took place at a level which – in one sense – has nothing to do with the participants, or their particular preoccupations, but it could not have happened without them.

As providers of the so-called 'occasional' services – weddings, baptisms, funerals and so on – the church finds itself called into many different situations. Those who have to provide these services can be left wondering what it was all about, as, for example, when faced with 3-year-olds being presented for baptism in order to gain places in church schools – an 'arid task' as one priest said, when there was no indication of any family commitment.

When it comes to funerals, many clergy value being asked to be part of a person's passage from this life to the next, but it is not always straightforward. How, for example, was a young curate to approach her follow-up visit after a funeral where the entire family occupied the front row of the church and laughed loudly throughout the service? More generally, what would be natural from the church's point of view – to pray for the person who has died – may jar on relatives who are looking for a ceremony to contain their grief and celebrate the dead person: prayers asking for their forgiveness may be experienced as positively offensive. Likewise the requirements of relatives may jar on the church representatives. A Roman Catholic priest, who feels it is important 'to take the deaths of lapsed and fringe people seriously', described the difficulties he faces in the variety of expectations when the family are not used to the way the funeral service is done, and introduce, or want to introduce, elements such as long eulogies or particular music that are not necessarily appropriate. 'You can say it is not normally done,' he said, 'and they accept that – or you can have a very negative reaction.'

These occasional services do, however, provide opportunities for the church to step into people's lives as a friend in need. Sally and her mother were cradle Anglicans who had long ago stopped going to church, but when Sally's mother was dying, she became concerned about her funeral and wanted to make sure it was taken by a priest. Through a friend, they contacted a priest who not only promised to take the funeral but offered to come and meet the dying woman. He spent time with her, and was able to talk about that meeting during the funeral service. He also continued to keep in touch with Sally by phone for several months afterwards. Sally went to church a few times after her mother died, but it did not hold any particular meaning for her and she has not continued. She will not, however, forget the kindness that that priest showed: he was there when needed, without strings, and faded from the scene when the job was done.

When my brother became terminally ill, the church again provided support without making any demands. My brother had not been near a church, apart from the family funerals, for many years. Our parents and uncles and aunts had all died, so there were no ongoing church connections through them. Nevertheless, the hospital chaplain regularly sat with him when he was ill in hospital, and a priest who had known our family for a long time visited more or less weekly through a harrowing process that lasted more than a year. When my brother was well enough, this priest would celebrate the Eucharist at his bedside. For various ecclesiological reasons none of the rest of us who were present at those Eucharists were able to receive communion, but during them all the tensions that surround caring for a dying person at home simply dissipated. Truly Christ was in our midst. For the last few weeks of my brother's life, our friend was unable to visit, but a local minister, who had never met any of the people involved, came into the situation. He visited several times, and eventually took the funeral with great sensitivity.

A therapist working in a hospice paid tribute to the importance of people rooted in their own belief – a priest, a rabbi, an imam or whatever – in helping to strengthen patients facing serious or terminal illness: 'We do need people who believe certain things.' The people who were really able to help were those who were sufficiently grounded not to cling too much to any particular dogma, and allow the patient's attitude to be exploratory. The important thing they demonstrated, he felt, was that 'it is all right to have a spiritual life – and it does not have to be a certain way'.

Jill's story

Our final witness for the defence is someone, whom we will call Jill, whose lifelong involvement with church has both widened and deepened her relationship with God and with other human beings. In her journey there is a remarkable fit between an internal conviction that God has a purpose for each of us, a natural propensity to pray and church life.

Jill, who is now in her sixties, discovered the church as a child. As with Celia, her first contact with church was through nuns at her convent day school, and she was deeply attracted by the gentleness of the nuns. At the same time, she envied the Catholic children at the school: 'I was desperate to go to church on Sundays like the Catholics at my school – and I desperately wanted a rosary.' The eldest of four children, at the age of ten she persuaded her parents and the rest of the family to begin going to the local Anglican church, and she was not disappointed: 'I got caught up in it. I loved everything about it.'

As time went on, the rest of Jill's family dropped out of church, but Jill continued, attending mostly Anglican and Baptist churches as she grew up, and there were a number of key figures in the churches who helped her develop a deep faith. Jill is inwardly convinced that God has a purpose for every person, and has a strong sense of being guided throughout her life. Although she is someone who naturally engages very easily at a social level, church is something far more than that to her: 'We are made in the image of God,' she said, 'and we are born with a God-shaped hole. We don't feel complete as people unless that hole is filled.' For her, then, the church is 'a gateway to the spiritual', a way for each of us to find our own path to God.

'Encouragement' is a word that Jill uses often about the church – practical as well as spiritual encouragement, and the importance of a shared outlook. 'When you are connected with a group of people,' she said, 'you encourage each other.' Her only 'off period', as she calls it, was during five years abroad, when her horizons were widening and there was all the freedom of living in a different country. She did not find a church community where she felt really at home: even so, she continued to go to church on Sundays, 'out of duty rather than wanting to'. Apart from those few years, what is striking about her relationship with church is that it is neither needy on her part nor exploitative on theirs, but more like a good marriage: 'the mutual society, help and comfort that the one ought to have of the other.'[3] It is not, of course, that there are no problems, but the problems are survivable together.

On Jill's return to England she settled in the town where she has lived for the last thirty years or so, and where she belongs to the local Anglican church. It was here she met David and fell in love. David had been previously married and divorced and this caused her some internal struggle, but the church community was very supportive of their relationship. They were not able to have a church wedding, which was difficult for her, but they did have a service of blessing, and the vicar's attitude made a great difference: 'He would have married us if he could.' David was also a devout Christian – 'we were completely of one mind' – and he was very engaged with the work of the church: so much so, in fact, that for the first year of their marriage she resented the amount of time it took him away from home in the evenings, especially as she was often working at weekends. Nevertheless, she valued the home group to which they both belonged, and once her son was born, the support group for mothers of young children was invaluable. She and David went on to work together on a number of church projects including Traidcraft and a catechetical group, and were part of a network of mutual support and encouragement.

During those years, I was sometimes a guest in their house. It was a time when I had rejected anything to do with church, and I was wary of Christians. All the same, I found myself impressed by the way in which Jill and David's faith appeared to be totally integrated with their home life without being in any way intrusive. Grace was said before meals as a matter of course, without fuss. Otherwise there was simply a background awareness that faith was at the centre of their lives: nothing was imposed on anyone else. This held true when their son stopped wanting to go to church when he was thirteen. David and Jill did not force the issue ('We had seen so many people forcing their children to go to church'); it seemed to them counter-productive. Today, Jill knows that he respects her beliefs and the fact that she prays for him, and is also interested in discovering what faith meant to his father. 'The rest', said Jill, 'is between him and God.'

Life changed dramatically for all of them when David became seriously ill. The church community provided practical help and supported them with prayer; following James 5:14, a group from the church also came to the house and prayed with him on more than one occasion. He recovered, but fell ill again, with what turned out to be a brain tumour, though it took some time to arrive at a diagnosis. David was clearly very ill, and could not cope with people coming to the house. Jill was under great stress at work, and their son, who was still at school, was doing exams. These were very dark days for Jill – 'a terribly lonely time' – and a real challenge to faith, where she cried out to God in a way she had never done before. Into this darkness the church introduced a glimmer of light in the form of a woman from the congregation who left a plant on her doorstep with a brief note. 'It was so encouraging,' Jill said, 'like a message from God to say "I'm still here".'

Since David's death, now some years ago, Jill has continued to be very much supported by the church community, but it is shared and mutual support. The church is there for her when she needs it, but she, too, helps to care for others who are ill or in trouble, and she served for six years as churchwarden. Through the church she has also been involved in a local project helping prostitutes, as well as one in Africa improving midwifery and neo-natal care services. The vicar himself, she said, has had 'a huge impact' on her life. He was 'superb' in helping her care for her mother who died three years ago, but he also keeps a spiritual focus: 'he sees deeply but simply into things' is the way Jill put it.

Ecclesiology – in the sense of one church being more 'true' than any other – does not feature in Jill's thinking. She relates to people of various denominations, and, she says, 'can find something in any church'. The ongoing structure of the Anglican liturgy – as is usually the case with anyone who takes part in liturgy over a long period – does, however, mean a great deal: 'There is so much in it, and it means different things at different times. It is something to fall back on.' Ecclesiology, in the sense that church matters, however, is central to her faith. Though she would agree that there are many spiritual paths, the importance of church for her is that it is a body – the Body of Christ – where people can work out together what their path is. 'Without that', she said, 'you can get too inward looking.' Eucharist, the sharing of bread and wine, is also very important, not so much a mystical experience as a reminder – in the doing – of what she is involved in.

Having said so much about Jill's positive relationship with the church, it is important to note that she is aware of problems, both at a local level and on the wider scene. 'I can see why churches put some people off,' she remarked. 'When I go somewhere I make an effort to meet people, but not everyone can do that, and people can feel very unwelcome.' She also finds the level of disunity very difficult, as well as the 'focus on things that aren't important', such as people's sexuality, and 'making big issues out of them'.

There is one further aspect of Jill's church membership that is interesting here, in that she has a large extended family who are not churchgoers. There have been a number of crises in the wider family in recent years, and they tend to turn to her in times of trouble: she has been involved both practically and through prayer. As Jill sees it, the church nourishes and supports her in this, and she then shares this support and nourishment with the wider family. In this way the body is extended beyond its own boundaries: it could be said that she is the church for them.

In Jill's life, of course, belonging to a church goes far beyond simply turning up on Sundays. It has become woven into the very fabric of her life, and her story demonstrates how being part of the church can mean becoming ourselves part of the Christian story, and allowing it to live here and now.

5

Witnesses for the prosecution

> We are looking for God too, but not necessarily in the places where the church has hidden him.[1]

Womb or tomb?

'Is the church a womb or a tomb?', asked an ordinand who was feeling somewhat stifled by her experience of training. Is it a place of mysterious new growth, or is it a place of death and decay? Christ's tomb was of course both: he rose as 'the first fruits of those who sleep' (1 Corinthians 15:20). Just as the grain of wheat that falls into the ground and dies brings forth new life, so there is a sense in which death itself gives birth to the resurrected Christ. Yet when people complain about faith being stifled rather than enhanced by church life, they are not in general talking about a fertile darkness that generates new life. They are not even talking about the boredom that can – healthily – set in with any repeated task, freeing the mind to go deeper. They are asking where the underlying life and message are to be found.

Peter has been organist of the same church for ten years. 'I'm thinking of moving churches,' he said: 'I've been doing the same things a long time. It is all very routine and rather a drudge: I have to force myself to wake up. There is a lot I like about the church, but I don't like what it is turning into – an increasingly dull routine where I turn up, speak to a few people and go away again. It is absolutely not what I want to do.'

'The less time I spend in church buildings, the healthier my spiritual life is,' said an Anglican priest. 'I go back because that is what I do, and I do seem to be able to help others have a more fulfilling inner life. The fact that it does nothing positive and occasionally feels negative to me doesn't matter.'

In some people's minds the church, having lost touch with the reality of people's everyday lives, is already condemned to a slow death. 'The bishop told me we are simply presiding over the inevitable decay,' remarked one Anglican priest, while a number of people whose lives are deeply embedded in the church have said to me that 'it simply has to disappear'. Yet we have seen that there are people for whom it still has a great deal of significance – or potential significance. Here we give space to a 'litany of complaint': some of the things that give rise to the anger that is only just under the surface among those whose experience is of a body falling far short of Christ's teaching. No claim is made for the justness of these criticisms, and as with all criticisms they say something about the people who make them as well as about the institution. They do, however, remind us of ways in which, as church, we perhaps lose sight of the call to be the living Body of Christ. The strength of feeling involved may, of course, indicate that there is still considerable life in the body.

'We pray together and we fall apart'

Conflict features strongly in almost anyone's experience of church, and is, of course, part of any community life. What people find disturbing, however, is when there seems to be no continuity between the prayer life of the body and what goes on the rest of the time. It is as though a contract is constantly broken, and the problems are rarely addressed. A common complaint is that it is only the people who are easily made to feel guilty who are asked to examine their own contribution to a particular problem – something they would probably do anyway – while those who are convinced of their own rightness are rarely challenged. 'If this church is a functioning community,' said a woman who had been the subject of a number of envious attacks, 'why is it all right for people to hate me? Shouldn't it be a spiritual issue that people are asked to address?'

'So much time is wasted at PCC meetings,' said one man, 'so much bitterness over absurd little things. People are just not willing to engage – it drains the whole point of it.' He described an episode where an argument on the PCC had led to what he described as 'intemperate' language. 'It was staggering,' he said, 'I just didn't want any part of it.' Another man, who was once a churchwarden, resigned after the vicar was extremely rude to a woman on the PCC during a meeting. 'She resigned,' he said, 'and I resigned in support. I was appalled by that vicar's behaviour – it was so un-Godlike. Then I got a letter from the bishop telling me I couldn't resign as churchwarden and that he would tell me when I could resign. I never went back.'

Jane, a lay pastoral worker, says she often unwittingly upsets people. 'I try to do something and it turns out that "somebody else always does it" – or more often it turns out that somebody else always does something that is not the same thing at all. I don't mean to tread on people's toes, but people are quick to take offence.' She added, 'People in churches definitely behave worse than non-believers. A non-believer always has the hope of being converted. But we have the message and twist it. That is much worse.'

Failing to understand its own message

If we take it that the gospels tell us of the life of Christ, who himself is the supreme revelation of God to humanity, we can regard our attempts to *be* church as the attempt to live according to what we read there. This requires not only a text, but also our ability to perceive it, not only with the ears or eyes of the body, but with the mind and heart. Only then can it be translated into the way we live our lives. Absorbing, teaching and preaching the Gospel are clearly central to the church's role, but how this is done is a major source of dissatisfaction.

'There is so much moralising,' said one person. 'A good preacher preaches to himself – what is this text telling me? us? But so often I feel I have been placed by the preacher on the far side of an argument – and then attacked for thinking things I would never have dreamed of thinking in the first place.'

A priest commented that much of what is said in church is counter-productive because it is centred on particular values that are not those of the Gospel.

Ellen described a service where the preacher ignored half the Bible reading ('the half that was the point') and only took what he wanted to take from it. 'He used it as a vehicle to insinuate all kinds of evil things about gay people. I was absolutely incensed.' Afterwards she tried to discuss it with her family who were also there – 'but no one else had heard it. They just said it was a beautiful sermon and laughed at me. But I know I heard what he was saying.'

Some people find it very hard to relate the wonder and simplicity of the Christian message to what they perceive as a narrow insistence on dogma. One man, who has a degree in theology and has also studied various mystical traditions in some depth, described the sermons at his local church: 'They seem to be surrounded by such extraordinary arguments and detailed prescriptions about belief and the way things happen. I find it irrelevant – and unattractive – when describing the supernatural world. Yet one is expected to believe all this when it is so far removed from the simplicity which is at the heart of Christianity.' For the more mystically inclined, even a good sermon interrupts the flow of the service. Others would go further and find any insistence on dogma positively off-putting. One woman said, 'I long for holiness, and I can see ritual carries that, but I'm fed up with people thinking they have the right to pontificate to other people about what's true and what isn't true.' Her experience was that spiritual honesty and a sense of wonder and connection was much more alive among ordinary people than in anything to do with the church. 'The church should be needing our holiness, drawing on our holiness,' she said, 'not telling us what's what.'

It is clear that poor preaching – or what is perceived as poor preaching – makes people angry. 'I went to six services at my local church,' said a woman who had recently moved house, 'hoping the standard of preaching might improve – that I had just caught it on a bad day. But it didn't. It is immensely frustrating that people are prepared to accept such a low standard of presentation – and at the same time ask why young people are not interested in church. I never want to step inside the place again, because the worship – their word not mine – is dire, and it makes me want to break things.'

Brenda, an Anglican priest, feels that not enough is done in training to encourage good preaching, and identified a core problem: 'You go through the C of E selection and then you are expected to grapple with "grown-up" theology – textual criticism, de-mythologisation and so on – but you are not expected to take any of that back into the parish. They educate the clergy in their critical faculties, but not the laity, so the laity become infantilised.' The clergy, that is, were meant on the one hand to wrestle with their own doubt, and the avalanche of critique which is modern theology, but on the other to convey the faith to the laity in straightforward terms. She also thinks that most preaching suffers from lack of preparation, not because the clergy are not willing, but because 'there is very little time or energy left over from admin and pastoral work'. She added, 'Thinking, praying and study are all considered rather elitist – so who is going to focus on education?' All this is related to what she sees as a far greater problem: that there is no place for the laity's experience of God in the world to be heard – 'We never allow lay people to speak of their own experience. It is the one thing lay people never do.'

One of Brenda's suggestions is that sermons could at least sometimes be shared with the laity: 'For this to happen a clergy person and a lay person need to meet to discuss the readings in good time and share their thinking about the passages together. Sometimes I have shared a sermon slot with the proviso that we each write down and share what we are going to say and stick to it. I see my role then as supporting whoever it is to have a voice. Church regulations mean that it really has to be a 'double act'. At other times I have spoken with someone and allowed them to inform my thinking, but they have not wanted an up-front role, though they might allow me to say that we had spoken and I was communicating their ideas and experience of life. I have also invited members of the congregation (not during the liturgy) to contribute to a discussion, and woven their ideas into a sermon. All these experiments have involved a great deal of work beforehand (much easier to do it myself!) – but when we have done it, it has always been greatly appreciated.'

A lay person from another church complained that sermons are preached *at* the congregation: 'Why should lay people not talk back and discuss what the preacher has said? Why can't we interrupt, argue, complain, disagree?' It is perhaps hard to imagine on this basis how one would ever get to the end of the service, but it does raise questions about the nature and function of sermons. Are they theological reflection by someone who, being a religious professional, has more background, theological expertise, and (at least in theory) time to do this effectively – or should they provide a forum for people to relate their experience to the faith, and discuss what they really believe?

Among the laity, however, lack of satisfaction is often associated not with a lack of interaction, but with lack of teaching. 'Poor sermons,' said one person who was otherwise quite satisfied with her church community, 'that's the real negative side. You go there to try to learn – and then it's not there.'

Jeffrey described how, as a member of a congregation largely composed of graduates like himself, he had been appalled by the lack of serious engagement with the Christian story. He engaged every day in Bible reading and prayer, and went regularly to the discussion groups. 'The answer was always Jesus,' he said. '"We're not like Jesus." "Should we be?" "Can we be?" It got so dull. The songs were like very simple mantras, simplistic, brainwashing. I tolerated it for a while, and even took a Jack and Jill confirmation test – but in two years I had done no studying with these people.'

At a church he attended some years later, there were three clergy who preached in rotation. One he described as very good. The second 'preached from the *Daily Mail* – right-wing bigotry and no content'. The third, he felt, was rather taken up with her own life narrative, but the crunch came in a sermon on Trinity Sunday, when she said, 'Jesus was a man so full of God he was God.' Jeffrey was in two minds whether to stand up and say, 'That is heresy.' He refrained from doing so because he was aware that the parish, being liberal in its views, had been called heretical by a neighbouring parish that was less liberal, and so the word would be misunderstood. His anger over the sermon, however, was primarily about the congregation being sold short of the riches of Christian theology. 'The ancient heretics', he said, 'did not understand the full beauty of the incarnation' – and this was also true of this particular preacher.

Jeffrey's experience is a curious mirror image of Brenda's complaint about the 'infantilisation' of the laity: in this case the lay person was better educated theologically than the ordained one. Eventually Jeffrey found himself contacting the vicar every three months to get a copy of the preaching rota, and ended up only going to church once a month. At another church he found that vestments of the correct liturgical colour would be put out for the priest 'by a team of old ladies', but when asked why he was wearing that colour that week he did not know. 'If he doesn't know, he shouldn't be wearing it,' commented Jeffrey. 'I would rather people just dropped it if they don't understand it.'

Even more fundamental than complaints about whether sermons are theologically sound is the sense that the gospel message is being missed altogether: not just by preachers but by congregations too: 'The core message of love, forgiveness and care for others needs to be heard. There is far too much propping up of the establishment. There is a radical message there and it needs to get through.' For a young priest – a college chaplain – this is the most important thing. 'If you take time to listen,' she said, 'we preach an extraordinary message which is too often buried under acrimony and prejudices and rows. People say the church is only interested in persecuting gays and women. I don't have any time for that sort of prejudice – but I do have time for the church. What we say is valuable and real, about hope, inclusion and radical transformation. I've not been able to find that anywhere else.'

'Worthy of his hire'? – working in the church

Although I enjoy leading workshops and retreats, I usually dislike being asked when the event is one organised by a church. This is because, with a few notable exceptions, churches are very bad at talking straight about money. A recent conversation was typical. I received a phone call asking me to lead a retreat over two days, involving three talks. Early on in our discussion, the organiser said, 'Of course, we'll pay your travel expenses [the venue was a cycle ride away], but I don't know if you require a fee.' I made no response to this, since I wanted time to think about it. The theme of the retreat appealed to me, and I was probably willing to do it anyway, but there is a lot of work involved in preparing three talks sufficient to provide enough material for two days' meditation. As we talked further, she dropped a number of remarks into the conversation, such as, 'Of course, it's only three talks'; 'With all your experience, there won't be very much work involved,' and so on. Irritated by this – and fully aware that preparing three talks is a major task – I decided that a fee was appropriate, and at the end of the conversation I returned to the subject and named my price. 'Of course,' she said, 'we are paying for your expertise' – as though paying me needed some kind of justification.

Inevitably the churches rely a great deal on voluntary work, and there is nothing wrong with this. What tends to happen, unfortunately, is that as soon as anyone demonstrates a degree of competence, the demands on them very quickly get out of hand. Jeffrey's story of a church he attended as a young man is typical: 'The liturgy at this church was wonderful, but pastorally it was not good. As a twenty-something male I was full of ideas and my time got harnessed for the good of the church. I got burnt out. The vicar wanted a successful church. He wanted copies of things that worked from books, news, etc. I put together all kinds of Power-point presentations and so on, and he would say, "That was a great service – another one next month then?" He wanted a monthly agenda because we were a funky youth church and anything successful had to happen regularly. It was great at first – I felt special – but I ended up feeling used. I had a full-time job, and no one cared that I was just knocking myself out keeping up with all this stuff.'

As a member of his church choir, John is under pressure to turn up to both the morning and evening service. He is in full-time work, and lives with a partner (she is a member of the same church), so his free time is very precious. People are very reluctant to accept that he can only be available for one Sunday service, and he experiences this as the church community refusing to reciprocate his own generosity – a common complaint, that it is impossible to be generous in church life because the demands are so great that any contribution you make is simply seen as falling short. What upsets John is that 'they could not accept that I *wanted* to come, but was only available for one service. How', he asked, 'do you approach your church community in a spirit of generosity, when more is taken than you want to or are able to give? You are not doing it for the gratitude, but you do end up feeling drained and criticised.'

As an adult convert, John, as we have seen in the previous chapter, has been deeply impressed by the way in which Christian theology can inform Christian behaviour. At times, however, his experience has been that overt criticism of things he has done for the church is not tempered by recognition of what he has given. The minister would pick on some small thing that had gone wrong, without paying any attention to the larger contribution which had gone right. He found this very difficult because it felt wrong not to defend himself against unjust criticism, but also wrong to defend himself in opposition to a minister in authority within the church.

Many problems over work and time can be put down to bad management, which, as John said, can have greater potential for causing distress in a church situation than in a paid job. 'If you are at work, you at least have the consolation that you are being paid – and if the exchange is no longer worthwhile you can bail out. When you contribute to your church community, however, you don't expect payment: you do it as a Christian, as part of living out your faith. When your contribution is criticised it comes as an added insult because it fails to recognise the voluntariness of your contribution. Your participation in church is undermined, and what should be a joyous activity becomes laborious and complex.'

John is clearly the kind of person to see through projects, and to approach them with a high degree of competence. A frequent problem encountered in church life, however, is investment not in getting the job done, but in the social value of being involved in the job. The unsuspecting volunteer hears that – say – there are problems about distributing the parish magazine, and offers to help. He then finds that an inordinate amount of his time is taken up, not by the distribution, which can be done in an hour or two, but by people ringing him up, often at unsocial hours, to introduce complications (e.g. the envelopes must be handwritten – 'computer-printed labels are *so* impersonal'), or expecting him to take part in last-minute crisis assembly work, and so on. There are, of course, extremely valuable projects that place the involvement of people above perfection in execution of the task. An enormous amount of frustration, however, is caused to busy people trying to keep the show on the road, when there seems to be an assumption that because a job is being done for the church, it can be done inefficiently, at the last minute and in crisis conditions, and that this is even socially desirable, fostering bonding in adversity. Yes, adversity can be bonding, but not when it appears to be created, almost deliberately, by the people one is supposed to be bonding with.

Then there is the fact that we all have to eat: if the church does not pay, someone else does. 'A labourer is worthy of his – or her – hire,' said a part-time teacher and church worker. 'There is a struggle to give willingly without any thought of return – but is this right? I've always viewed my work as my contribution to society, but at times have yearned to make a wage and felt guilty about family financial support for my uncommercial activities.'

If the situation is bad for lay people, it can be far worse for the professionals, who are often expected neither to have personal needs nor to give any time to their families. A tutor in a theological college worked out that out of the sixty hours a week required by his contract, by the time he had fulfilled all his core commitments, but before he had opened a letter or answered the telephone, he could expect to spend forty-three minutes a week alone in his study. A woman about to be ordained went to meet her prospective vicar. Since she had a husband and a small daughter she asked whether she could adjust her working hours so as to be home in the early evenings two nights a week. Permission was refused.

An Anglican priest of some twenty-five years' standing was only a few years off retirement when his wife was diagnosed with cancer. The doctors thought she had about five years to live. Suddenly there was no retirement together to look forward to, and the couple decided that in order to make the most of the time left to them, the husband would apply to work part-time. He was prepared to be flexible, to relocate to any part of the country, and of course to be paid only a part-time salary. It was not realistic for him to think in terms of stopping work altogether. He made numerous applications, and contacted anyone he could think of who might be able to help. The answer was always the same. He was welcome to go part-time, but could not expect to be paid anything at all unless he was prepared to remain full-time. Finally, with much regret, he found a part-time job as a Baptist minister.

It is to be fervently hoped that the question of paying part-time clergy will be resolved in the Anglican Church, not only because of cases like this one, but because of the anger it arouses in the husbands and wives of clergy who see their spouses doing hard and skilled work for the church with no payment. The family pays twice – in the mother or father's commitment of time and energy to the church – and in the lack of income.

The plight of a woman who questioned this practice when taking up her title post raises issues that – whether or not this situation changes – are pertinent to many clergy. She began by trying to specify how many hours a week were expected from her as a part-time curate, and was staggered to be told that if she needed to specify the hours she worked, then she was not sufficiently committed to take up a stipendiary post. As she said: 'The hours I was specifying – if anyone had bothered to consider them – are a sign of my commitment. The time I was safeguarding was time for my family and time to keep my household in order – but I was relinquishing practically all the time that would have been for myself or my own relaxation. Now it appears that even if I give up any expectation of remuneration the church considers it has the right to ask for more than I can easily give without once again compromising the needs of my family.'

Because her family did not want to go through the disruption of a move to a full-time stipendiary post, which would have affected both her husband's job and her children's schooling as well as forcing them to become a 'vicarage family' which they did not want to be, she was told that she would have to work for nothing. 'I feel that no one is listening to me when I try and explain that my family has claims on me too, and that these must be honoured.' She felt trapped, betrayed and let down. 'I keep thinking it is God I am rebelling against when really it is just an outmoded and inadequate institution. It is crucial to my ability to carry on that I believe God is with me in this – so God ends up being somewhere other than the church and that doesn't feel right either.'

Honesty, vision and sensitivity?

Somehow we like to think that people who are involved in the church – in prayer and the gospel story – might show the effects of this in their attitude to the world and the way they relate to others. What is so often experienced, however, is that it is difficult to trace a connection. Whatever church discipline may be, and whatever necessity there may be to observe it, the way in which problems are approached is often a cause of greater distress than the problems themselves. We are not talking here about the way in which great or particularly artistic or holy people can be difficult to live with, but with what appears to be a lack of what one might call 'joined-up living'.

'As a child I really loved the church,' said Rebecca, a clergy daughter, 'I really loved it. I loved the feeling that it was striving for something. There was so much beauty – the boys in the choir, the robes, the candles, the shining things. There was mystery and it was available there – and it all went.' When asked what had changed, she described an event which had been definitive for her around the age of fourteen when she was inspired by the project to rebuild Coventry Cathedral. 'I was fired with the vision of peace, of reconciliation, of something new coming out of the old after the bombing, of incorporating art. I wanted to do something really significant towards it, and I was told I could buy a brick with my pocket money. It was such a vision, and they said "Buy a brick".' The sense of opportunity missed had persisted in a number of adult attempts to become a churchgoer: 'There is no sense of communal worship. It is like a club, an excuse for laziness and a lack of holiness. You don't have to strive.'

Many people are looking for someone who is really willing to talk openly about spiritual matters – not in pious or easy terms, but really looking at how what we believe – or might, or can't believe – relates to our everyday lives. To do this in ways that allow for people's doubts and difficulties takes a certain kind of courage, and while there are some people within the churches who are very gifted as spiritual directors and guides, the churches in general do not have a good reputation in this regard. A typical example is someone who came to me for counselling some years ago wanting to explore how her depression related to spirituality. 'The vicar doesn't talk about these things,' she said. Another person remarked, 'I would not have thought to ask the vicar for spiritual guidance: he was not that kind of priest, though he was a nice guy.'

Considering the remarkable work that is done by so many clergy, it may seem churlish to raise these comments here. But there is, sadly, a perception that many clergy do not really engage with either the spiritual or the emotional aspects of life. This can be a question of managing the very complex role of being both part of a community and in a very special position within it. 'I wouldn't consider going to the clergy with my personal problems,' said a young Catholic, who thought of the clergy she knew as 'Mummy's tame priests': 'The priest at the church where I grew up was very lively – cheery and practical. My mother befriended him and he came to the house for meals and so on. But you can hardly dole out the vegetables and then start in on your problems – it doesn't seem fair.'

Role is, of course, a very strange thing. I sometimes see myself switch to being a caring, sensitive person in role, when I would be as difficult as can be out of it. There are also times when I see myself being cold and authoritative in role, when out of it I would be caring and friendly. There are many criticisms, however, about the general bearing of some clergy, as though they are somehow cut off from reality. 'The vicar came round when my wife died,' a man said, 'and he laughed. I said to him, "This is serious, you know, what's going on here".' 'The vicar came to visit my father when he was dying,' said a young woman. 'He was very nice – but, oh dear. These people always seem as though they would be so much happier doing something else.' 'There is a lack of getting to grips with the world among the clergy,' said another. 'They are hiding. They all walk the same.'

A side-effect of over-identification with the role, and the lack of self-awareness that goes with it, is sometimes a simply appalling carelessness in dealing with people, at a level well below what we would generally find in the surrounding culture. For example, a young ordinand who was permanently disabled and spent most of his life in a wheelchair was contacted by a senior priest who needed to visit him in order to report on how his training was progressing. He was understandably distressed when the senior man phoned and announced he would arrive the following morning. 'You won't mind, I hope,' he added heartily, 'if I am in my running shorts? I'm in training for a marathon.' Perhaps an honest remark, but hardly sensitive.

The complaints we make are often not so much to do with what the church believes or its practices, as with this other level of being – where is the vision? Where is the courage to take risks? Where is the honesty? Where is the sensitivity to others?

Michael's story

From an early age, Michael was aware that he was gay, but since his church life generally took place in liberal surroundings, he did not experience the level of anxiety about being gay that many church people do. Also, since he comes from a family who sent the children to church but did not go themselves, and there was not much interplay between church and day-to-day life, perhaps this helped him to separate out his sense of himself as a gay man from what the church might expect. When he left home he continued going to church as a university student, and lived in an Anglican chaplaincy where he met his first partner, who is now a priest.

It was at university that Michael began to wonder what he was doing in church. He went through a very rebellious phase: turning up drunk to services, saying outrageous things out loud during them, and so on. 'I enjoyed being naughty,' admitted Michael, but looking back he felt there were two significant aspects to his behaviour: 'It was challenging myself, and at a deeper level it was asking, "Is there anyone there?" ' Michael was an organist, and although the services themselves did not by this time mean a great deal to him, playing for them did, and it was when he was playing for services that he got the sense of a response: 'I got the sense that there was something, and I didn't relate the two [church and this 'sense of something']. I realised that for me, if I had any kind of relationship with God it was being on my own with it.' He stopped going to church for a very long time, and although he still goes to church from time to time he often finds it difficult to reconcile services with spiritual experience: 'I know it sounds judgemental,' he said, 'but I look at all these people and think, "What *are* you doing here?" It is almost as if they are going because that is just what you do, and for me that gets in the way.'

In spite of his rebellion – or perhaps the rebellion was in part a response to it – Michael felt the stirrings of a vocation to ordination. He experienced great internal resistance to this: 'The only way was to ignore it and pull away from it.' All the same, a spiritual search has remained central in his life and work: 'I don't know how you separate your beliefs and spirituality from who you are,' he said; but he remained angry with the church's insistence on dogma and its exclusivity, and found himself 'wanting to find that destructive part of myself and really break it apart'.

Nevetherless, the sense of vocation to ordination survived all Michael's best efforts to ignore it, and at the age of forty-five he began to investigate the possibility of putting himself forward. His approach was welcomed, and he was sent to see a Diocesan Director of Ordinands, with whom he had a series of interviews. Things were progressing well, and they had some helpful and honest discussions. Then, one day, he asked her about how his sexuality would affect the selection process, and she replied, 'When they ask you about your sexuality, just lie.' For Michael, that was the end. 'Absolutely not,' he said. 'I am forty-five years old, I have been gay all my life, and how can you just lose part of yourself?' For him the issue at stake was not the church's attitude to homosexuality, but its dishonesty, and he was both hurt and angry. He accepted that the church had problems with his sexuality – that was why he asked the question – but his sense of shock resulted from being expected to lie about who he was. 'If people in authority think that's OK then actually there is something really wrong. They want you to deny a huge part of yourself, and I just don't want to belong to an organisation that can do that to people: that can say "It is wrong to be who you are, so don't tell us who you are. Just work for us."'

The sense of betrayal was almost overwhelming, and behind Michael's continuing anger with the church lies a deep wound: 'I feel really hurt by it and it feels as though that will never be able to be healed.' 'I could have gone in and tried to change it,' he added, 'but I've got more important battles. That's not my battle.' He now lives in a registered partnership with a man who was brought up as a Roman Catholic. 'He doesn't go to church, said Michael, 'but he still has inbuilt in him, "If you do that you'll go to hell." To me that is absolutely ridiculous – yet he lives his life like that.'

Besides the personal hurt, Michael's concern is that this everyday level of functioning is being acted out in a huge arena, where the church is about segregation, not integration. 'You can't separate parts of you into boxes,' he said, 'and if we can't do anything on an everyday level it is hopeless.' In spite of this, Michael continues to work with – and challenge – the various churches he comes in contact with in his work as a therapist in a hospital – and to be involved in organising services on special occasions. He values shared worship, and continues to be moved by people coming together to sing Christian hymns, seeing music and story as the most positive contribution of Christianity to society. Personally, however, it looks likely that he will remain on the fringes of any church.

'It's my church'

As Christians we talk a great deal about inclusion and acceptance, and there is no doubt that many, many Christians practise these and are healing presences in the world as a result. To do so, however, requires a certain openness to experience, a certain vulnerability, and church can be a place where, far from opening ourselves up, we surround ourselves with defensive structures.

We have seen how important a sense of welcome can be to people approaching the church, especially when this is provided sensitively, with a light touch. Many visitors to churches find, however, that there is no such thing. 'Sadly the good church stories are hugely outnumbered by the bad church stories,' a priest acknowledged. 'I've seen and heard it so many times: someone comes in very tentatively, looks around, maybe gives a little smile, sits down – and then is immediately pounced on by someone who says, "You can't sit there – that's Mrs So-and-So's place." ' A hospital worker said that most of his experience of church had been 'about feeling unwelcome. What disturbs me', he went on, 'is how unwelcoming churches can be compared with my place of work. There are many times I have been to church and absolutely no one speaks to me. It seems odd. But you are either part of it or you are not, and to become part of it takes a huge amount of energy. I can't be bothered. I already have friends – I don't need the church socially.'

A Catholic priest celebrated a weekday Mass at a suburban church. There were a number of elderly, retired people there, but it was also the day when teenagers from the local school came and took part. He was impressed and delighted by the way these schoolchildren participated in reading the lessons, serving at the altar and so on, and remarked on this afterwards to one of the elderly parishioners. 'Yes,' he replied gloomily, 'they are taking over our church.'

At a PCC meeting in an Anglican parish, there was a discussion as to whether they should sign an 'Inclusive Church' petition affirming gay and lesbian people as full members of the Church.[2] A member of the PCC who had always seemed liberal in her views said, 'I won't vote against signing the petition provided you can guarantee we won't get any of those sort of people in our church who might want to work with our children.' When pressed as to what she meant, she responded, 'Well, they are not safe with our children are they – they are paedophiles.' The parish priest – herself a lesbian – was understandably shocked. 'In so many congregations,' she said, 'the last thing they actually want is mission and evangelism – they are very happy the way they are thanks very much, and they don't want anybody coming in. In fact,' she added, 'I think for most of them Jesus was the last sort of person they would want to welcome into the church.'

When it comes to exclusivity practised *between* the churches, this can be even more incomprehensible to ordinary human beings than the exclusive attitude churches sometimes appear to have to outsiders. There may be serious ecclesiological reasons behind the boundaries that are set, but they generally involve a sophisticated level of understanding that is inaccessible to the ordinary churchgoer.

An example occurred shortly after I had been received into the Orthodox Church. My husband and daughter – both baptised Anglicans but neither of them churchgoers – were not received although they came to the service. My daughter was nine at the time, and a keen cook, so when someone offered to show me how the *prosphora* (small loaves baked for the liturgy) were made, I was delighted, not least because it was a church activity my daughter would enjoy. These *prosphora* are made from ordinary bread dough, shaped in a particular way, and stamped with a wooden stamp before baking. People buy them before the liturgy and give them in to the sanctuary, along with the names of people they would especially like to be remembered. They are not used in communion, but are blessed, and at the end of the liturgy are brought back into the main church to be shared. The regular maker of *prosphora*, my daughter and I spent a very pleasant afternoon, and the next day I told another parishioner about it. I was stunned to discover that this person was genuinely shocked because the hands of a non-Orthodox (albeit a baptised Anglican) child had been involved in making the *prosphora*.

James is an Anglican married to a devout Catholic, and they have had many serious discussions about where they stand with the churches, the baptism of their children and so on. For some while he went with his wife to the local Catholic church, but stopped, put off not so much that he was not allowed to receive communion, but by the exclusive nature of the preaching: 'It almost seemed to say that anyone who was not a Catholic was not a Christian' (a criticism that is by no means limited to the Catholic Church!). He has never seriously considered becoming a Catholic himself, because his experience is of something far too prescriptive, even if there are preachers 'who can incorporate anything and everything into the Christian framework in a very inclusive way'.

Frances's story (2)

When we last met Frances, she had begun going to church after an encounter with the nuns she sought out after a series of bereavements. As time went on, she came up against the exclusivity in two ways – at a personal and at an ecclesial level.

In attending services, Frances found herself drawn more and more into 'a spiritual depth – something beyond psychology' and she began to meditate regularly. One Holy Week she became involved deeply in a meditation to which she returned each morning: it culminated in a powerful personal experience of Christ, which was like nothing she had ever felt before in her life: 'There were no words. Love poured down into me – *me*, Frances.' It was almost overwhelming, particularly for someone who was in the early stages of spiritual exploration, and she tried to discuss it with a number of people. Her voice broke as she said to me, 'You have to be so careful.' When she tried to share openly with others about her experience, the response from members of the congregation was 'How dare you?', and the priest told her it was not real: 'You don't feel that kind of thing.' Members of another church group said, 'That can't possibly happen to Frances.' In the end it was the sisters at the convent who validated her experience. One quite simply told her, 'You have had a conversion experience,' and another, 'When things get bad for you, never forget that' – advice which she was to remember and draw on some time later when she was diagnosed with cancer.

Meanwhile, Frances was drawing deeply on Orthodox liturgy, and was being encouraged to be received into the church. Although she had been confirmed into the Church of England as a child, she had never received communion, and did not understand why people thought it important that she should. 'I had never experienced such spiritual depth in a place,' she said. 'I could open myself up to it and I was as much a part of it as anyone there.' As she allowed herself to be persuaded towards being received, 'the old misgivings and criticisms began to interfere'. In particular she had great difficulty with the way in which she experienced the attitude to women. For example, boy children who were baptised were taken into the sanctuary before being returned to their mothers; girl children were not – and women were not allowed into the sanctuary at all.

Frances was confused by this. She was told that the church should embrace all, but 'if I could feel that love from Christ as a professed atheist,' she said, 'why cannot women be allowed into the sanctuary?' It seemed that the price of the deeply spiritual liturgy was cultural baggage that she could not reconcile with being a twentieth-century Western woman. Like so many other traditions, there seemed to be no theological basis to the practice, only a resistance to change. There were 'terrible arguments' but in the end she decided the only way to confront the problems was by joining.

This was where she encountered a – to her – bewildering response at the institutional level. She was asked who would be her sponsor, and naturally she thought of the Roman Catholic sister who had been her spiritual guide and friend ever since she had knocked on the door of the convent years before, and who had introduced her to Orthodox worship. She was appalled and puzzled to be told this was not possible. Although the attitude of the church in this respect is completely understandable from an ecclesial point of view, the point here is that to Frances, church was church, and it was incomprehensible to her that she should not be accompanied on her journey by the person who had brought her back into church. In spite of great personal conflict she was eventually received and began to receive communion, which, somewhat to her surprise, was 'a real experience'.

The violent undertow of religion

As St John says at the end of his gospel about the things that Jesus did, if every one of the complaints we have about church life were to be written, 'I suppose that the world itself could not contain the books that could be written' (John 21:25). If we look at the gospels, this should hardly surprise us. Christ himself says, 'Those who are well have no need of a physician, but those who are sick; I came not to call the righteous, but sinners' (Mark 2:17). He knows very well what we are like, and that is what makes the incarnation – choosing to be one of us – so remarkable.

In following Christ it is natural – like James and John – to want to be on the winning side. The problem is that God is on everyone's side, at a level which it takes a lifetime to begin to comprehend, and we constantly appropriate him to shore up our own religious positions, which have very little to do with relating to God. This was brilliantly illustrated by *The Now Show* (BBC Radio 4).[3] They broadcast an appeal on behalf of the world's atheists to the monotheistic religions, asking them to stop blowing up the planet while preaching peace. We, the atheists, they said, don't have an afterlife like you. This planet is all we have got and we want it back. The effect of religion in this world was an increase of violence: if only all the religious people could stop fighting each other the world would be a more peaceful place. In a brilliant follow-up the next week, they showed how this rallying call had turned atheism itself into a religion. The 'atheist' has been drawn into religious practice, arousing the crowd to call together on 'Hu-*man*', with a view to going out and fighting against the religious people. No one, they seemed to be reminding us, is free from the religious instinct – and it is both seductive and dangerous.

One can, of course, believe in God and keep away from any kind of institutionalised religion, but as soon as we share belief, prayer and so on with others, however, we begin to institutionalise, even if only in a very small way. We see the problems this creates right from the beginning of the Acts of the Apostles. For this reason we cannot afford not to ask the questions that distinguish church from other activities and groups. Being church, trying to live according to the Gospel, is an ongoing process of deepening our understanding, with many deviations along the way – as was also true for the original disciples. If it were not so, there would be no point in revelation, because we would know everything already.

When we see the church falling short of the gospel message we can, and should, complain – not because the church is our enemy, but because *we* are the church! Each of us is on a journey, in which we can be helped by others, present and past, who have trodden the same path, but in which each can only ultimately learn the way for him- or herself. At best the church provides a body of experience which guides us in roughly the right direction, though, being human, we are infinitely capable of misinterpreting what is in front of us – institutionally as well as individually.

6

When the event is mightier than the structure

In a lecture given in London in 1991, Dr Murray Cox, who was at the time a consultant psychiatrist at Broadmoor, asked, 'When the event is mightier than the structure, how do we cope?'[1] This question, particularly coming from someone in his position, struck me as an extraordinarily useful one – applicable in a great many situations. Later in his talk, he made the point that psychotherapy can be usefully supportive when the external world is too harsh, or helpfully confrontational when it is important to confront the patient's relationship with him- or herself. He compared this with Christ saying on the one hand, 'Come *unto* me [and I will give you rest]' and 'Come *follow* me' (i.e. do what I do and take up your cross), and suggested that the task of healing involves a balance between these two. There are times when we simply need what the priest in the last chapter called 'a haven of kindness' – and in a sense we need this all the time if we are to grow and thrive – but there are other times when we need people who will have the courage to challenge our ways of thinking, and help us look at what we ourselves are contributing to a problem.

If the church is to be a healing presence in the world, then a balance between these two is certainly needed. It must work to maintain a compassionate attitude both to its own people and those outside, and at the same time it cannot afford to become a comfort zone, where there is no stimulus to growth, or, indeed, repentance – becoming what one clergy daughter called 'a lazy game of purity and love and spirituality'.

A church structure that is working well is integrated with what its members believe, in such a way that this provides both containment and challenge. Putting Christ at the centre is experienced as a common task requiring serious commitment and prayer. There is a coherence between belief and practice, spiritual nourishment through the services and the sacraments, teaching and pastoral care, and a sufficiently strong community to contain difference and disagreement, and make room for visitors and newcomers. At the same time, a functional church community looks beyond itself, and avoids getting bogged down in its everyday quarrels and concerns. Hopefully it will contribute in some way to the surrounding secular community, and be aware of its wider connections: both throughout the ordinary world, and with the unseen world beyond space and time with the unseen world, stretching back into the past and looking to the future.

The functioning church also provides a *temenos* – or container – for the spiritual life of its members, which can allow for personal growth and spiritual exploration.

What happens, however, when 'the event is mightier than the structure' – when outside pressures, internal changes, or difficulties within the church community itself, mean that church life is no longer serving its purpose in an individual's life? The same question applies as in any intimate relationship – is the container sufficient? There are a number of ways in which it can become impossible for a church to respond adequately to events: changes in the church itself; a lack of fit between church and cultural identity; internal change in a person which means the church becomes no longer meaningful; or events in a person's life where the church structure proves insufficient.

In this chapter we will take stories that illustrate each of these situations, and, in the light of the gospel story, explore ways in which we react.

Changes in the church itself

A very obvious example of a change in the church itself comes from the ordination of women in the Anglican Church, and the controversy over women bishops. It should by now be clear that I myself have no difficulty with the ordination of women, and applaud the fact that after the terrible battles of the 1990s, the current generation of women priests are, as one put it, 'walking through an open door'.

I am also, of course, aware that there are people who are deeply distressed by this development, and who have left the Anglican Church as a result. What is interesting, however, is when we see the problem not so much as whether or not women should be ordained, but as one of what the church actually believes. George was for many years an Anglican priest, but became a Roman Catholic when women began to be ordained to the priesthood. This was not because of the ordination of women as such, but because of the decision to allow for the so-called 'dual integrity' (a contradiction in terms, surely!) whereby the Anglican Church simultaneously ordained women as priests and acknowledged that for some people this was unacceptable. It led to some very strange and painful situations, such as at one theological college where I taught, where the daily Mass was celebrated one day each week by a woman. The principal himself, though responsible for the training of women for the priesthood, refused to receive communion on these occasions, and there was even a second Mass on that day each week for others who felt the same! As one woman priest – a curate in an Anglo-Catholic parish where a number of people chose to stay away from Mass when she was celebrating – put it at the time: 'It is true to say that women are the only group of people actively legislated against by the church. The words 'two integrities' enshrine and permit discrimination. We would all protest if people were given a rota to avoid black or gay priests but the option of the choice to avoid women has been a weekly reality for me.'

It was not even this aspect which primarily concerned George, however. The decision to have 'two integrities' meant for him that the church was not saying women should be ordained, but 'The ordination of women is OK if you believe it.' It upset his whole perception of the ecclesial structure of the church built around the Eucharist: 'It was the key thing that undermined me as an Anglican,' he said, 'that the sacraments should be a matter of guesswork, of private opinion.' This was the sticking point. It was the importance of the unity of the sacraments that persuaded him to be received into the Roman Catholic Church.

For Fred, who is still an Anglican priest, the problem is a little different. He believes fervently that the ordination of women is wrong, and has considered moving to the Roman Catholic Church. But, he told me, if he were to do so he would have to state that Anglican Orders were invalid. This is something he would never be prepared to do: it would undermine his whole experience as a priest of thirty years' standing. His sense of there being 'no hiding place' after the recent decisions over women bishops is very real.

The culture gap: a lack of fit between church and cultural identity

Culture and church life are deeply intertwined. As we see with the Orthodox, the Catholics and the Anglican Communion, when large population movements take place, and with the ease of global communication, disparate groups are thrown together to the extent that each can simply find it impossible to recognise church as they understand it in the other. Inevitably splits take place.

For years I was part of a UK diocese of the Russian Orthodox Church, and one of the things that made this meaningful for many of our members during the years of communist oppression was that this particular spiritual tradition was not only being kept alive, but being allowed to live and evolve, in ways that were simply not possible at the time in Russia and Eastern Europe. When communism fell, the new-found freedom of the church was of course a marvellous thing – but it then became virtually impossible for many of us to straddle the cultural gap between the church life we had lived in the West for almost a century and the expectations of a church that had been underground throughout that time. They could not accept many aspects of church life as it appeared to them in this country: we could not be expected to go back in time.

Church and culture can also be irreconcilable at a personal level, and it was this that was 'mightier than the structure' for Frances, whom we saw entering the Orthodox Church in the last chapter.

Frances's story (3)

As we have seen, Frances's mystical side was fed deeply by Orthodox liturgy, and to her surprise she found that entering the church and receiving communion went beyond what she had experienced as an outsider. She had few illusions about the culture gap between herself and the church community at large, but she believed there would be room for change within it. As we have seen, from a child Frances had had difficulty with the story of Adam and Eve, and how in Christianity in general it can be used as an excuse to think of women as second-class citizens: 'The Roman Catholics and the Orthodox use it to keep women in their place,' she remarked. As the day of her reception into the Orthodox Church grew closer, her internal conflict deepened: 'I needed to draw closer to Christ, but I had real misgivings about the place of women. I came from a long line of strong-minded women and men who supported them. I kept asking myself: which is more important – drawing close to Christ, or the problems with women?' Once within the church she wanted 'to raise women's awareness of their own worth', and found that other women there were keen for her to address women's issues: 'Do something,' they said, 'and we will support you.' It was however a losing battle.

Frances also found it hard to cope with attitudes to divorce, abortion and homosexuality, and she was appalled one day to hear a priest say in a sermon that depression was a sin. 'One of the things I found totally unacceptable', she said, 'was that when I challenged these things I was told this is how it has always been. How could they say that, when we are living here and now, in a Western society?' Finally she left the church. 'I had to do it,' she said, 'I had to make it very clear I had left. I could not condone the practices.' Today Frances remains outside the church and does not go to communion, though she retains close friends within it, and still values being able to be at services.

Whatever we may think of Frances's take on the church approach to certain issues, her story is of interest to us in the sense that here was a person of great honesty and integrity who could not bridge the gap between the way in which she understood her own life and that of people around her, and the way of looking at these things within the church. For her there was – and is – great spiritual depth in the worship, but the overall structure was insufficient to contain her identity as a twenty-first-century woman. Like many others, she could not reconcile her belief that Christ welcomes all and that the church is for everybody with the cultural attitudes she found there.

Such difficulties are not, of course, confined to the Orthodox Church but exist across the whole spectrum of church life, just as liberals – and strong women! – exist within Orthodoxy. Jeffrey's first church, for example, was a curious mixture of evangelicalism, charismatic revival and formal liturgy. Having been a very keen convert, Jeffrey became more and more restless, finding it difficult to relate being 'in' the church with the reality of life outside. He recalled a particular occasion when a young curate, a man in his thirties who was the father of three children, preached on abortion as a sin. Jeffrey's response was: 'One in three women has had an abortion. You cannot use the word "sin" in that context. You know nothing of the people you are talking to.' It seemed to him simple arrogance for a man who knew very little of people's lives to preach in this way.

Jeffrey has featured a number of times in the book so far. Here we tell his story as an example of how internal change can be an event that is mightier than the structure the church provides.

Internal change: Jeffrey's story

Jeffrey is a computer expert in his early forties, and we have already seen that he cares about sound theological teaching in the previous chapter. Jeffrey's family were not churchgoers, though both he and his sister were baptised as babies, and it was at the age of about seven that he first became aware of the existential dilemma of human existence. His mother was urging him one evening to get on with his homework, and when he asked why, she told him that it was in order to do well at school and go to university. Again he asked why, and was told that if he went to university he would stand a better chance of getting a good job. 'You mean', he asked, 'that that is all – you go to school, university and work and then you die?' 'Well, yes,' said his mother, and from then on he was always wondering if there was more.

His first real encounter with church was through a computer magazine which organised a summer camp when he was about twelve. It turned out to be a church camp, in which he was the only one who was not religious, although he belonged to cubs and scouts, and went to the occasional service. Eventually Jeffrey did make it to university, and it was there his real interest in church began: 'In my second year I met some Christian people who were kicking around, and they were very nice and friendly, and that was my introduction to church.' It was not initially clear to him what he was doing there: 'I didn't get the worship thing. I was always looking sideways at people and wondering what was going on with them – and what was supposed to be going on with me.'

Nevertheless, he stayed, and for seven years after leaving university he attended an evangelical church in a town where there was a lot of employment for recent graduates, so there was a new intake of young people every year. 'We became adults together,' he said, 'and it worked well.' Like the others he engaged in daily Bible reading and prayer at home, and the peer group was extremely supportive, and kept in close contact when he had to go to the other end of the country for two months on a work placement. On his return, however, Jeffrey became increasingly uncomfortable with both the particular church, and church in general: 'Questioning was not encouraged because danger lay in the questions, not in truth and certainty. For years I wondered what was wrong with me – and then I realised I'm OK. They were the ones who were mad. It was for me a period of great psychological growth. I found myself turning up there twice on Sundays. Towards the end I found myself wondering what else I would do on a Sunday. This was my pattern, and I had some anxiety as to what else I would do.'

For a while he stayed away, but one Sunday evening he went back, and at the end of the service approached the vicar and asked, 'Can I take communion?' He was given it from the reserved sacrament. Looking back, Jeffrey found this a very strange incident, and is perhaps a good example of the gulf that often exists between laity and clergy. Jeffery seems to have seen the vicar as someone capable of providing a particular service, and the vicar to have seen Jeffrey as someone whose needs he could fulfil, but it does not seem to have occurred to either of them to talk about what happened. 'It was very odd – bizarre,' said Jeffrey. 'What was it made me ask? And why did he accept so readily? Why in that style of church would it have occurred to me to ask? I don't know what came over me. It wasn't part of the culture, which was Bible, sing, and a moralistic sermon.' It was a time, he admitted, when he had started to wonder about the sacraments and to think there must be something more to church life than what he was used to. 'It was partly psychological maturing and getting older, but also looking deeper.'

The boundaries of that particular church community were very tight, so at first Jeffrey was at a loss as to what to do: 'You don't think about other ways of doing church when you are told yours is the church that has got salvation – so everyone else is suspect, alien.' Even when he moved to another town he first of all went to a service at a similar church: 'When I came away, my feeling was – this is the sort of place I have come from, not the place I am going to.' Whether he liked it or not, he realised that this was no longer the place for him.

After that he attended many different churches, sometimes over long periods of time. The church that made the greatest impression on him at this time was one which had a huge statue of Christ the King, with arms outstretched, blessing, and he was struck by the contrast between this and the bleeding, dying Christ that had dominated his previous church: 'The whole of that first service I kept looking at his hands, and I went back and photographed them later. The way the light came in and played on the hands was beautiful – and the image said something important about the contrast between where I had been and where I was going – it marked a change.'

After ten years as a committed Christian, however, he found it more and more difficult to find a church where he could express his faith. He had found evangelicalism too shallow – 'I'm happy, happy, happy, 'cos God's my daddy, daddy, daddy and he loves me, loves me, loves me' – Anglicans too casual about theology, Catholicism too liturgically impoverished, and Orthodoxy too counter-cultural. His theological understanding deepened: he took a postgraduate degree in theology, and he developed a sense of connection with many of the early church fathers.

The longing for God, meanwhile, became an urgent matter. 'Where can I go,' Jeffrey asked himself eventually, 'where I can draw a line in the sand in front of my God?' He was someone who was 'petrified' by silence, but he decided that he needed to 'stand on the edge and look into the abyss'. Even thinking about it he was full of dread, and a sense that the God he said he believed in was not real. Talking with a friend about this, he discovered that at least he was not alone: she began to cry. When he asked her why, 'she said she was crying with relief that there was someone who knew about this need.'

Since he had not found God in the parish churches, then, Jeffrey decided to visit a convent, and pray and fast for the weekend. 'I went to meet God that weekend, and if he did not show up that was it – I would throw it all away.' He also hoped that among the sisters he would meet someone who 'would tell me all the answers to life'. On arrival he was met by a nun who was extremely welcoming, but as is so often the case, he found it difficult to start asking the questions he needed to ask: 'How do you say to a nun, "Can I talk to you about God-stuff?" I don't know how you broach the subject.'

In fact, however, the nun did talk to him about prayer in ways he found helpful. She also 'won him over with home cooking, food, sleep and tea'. He felt like Elijah being fed by the raven, and though he 'didn't get the whirlwind' (cf. Job 38:1), the experience of ordinariness and the meeting of basic human needs in the convent was spiritually nourishing. His problem was far from solved: there was nothing so simple as a yes or a no, but he had in some sense met God – in a much more matter-of-fact way than he had imagined. What to do with the experience was, of course, another matter: his longing for spiritual encounter was by no means unusual, but how was it to relate to church life itself? The convent was part of the church, certainly, but he did not feel called to the monastic life. The search continued.

As time went on, Jeffrey's internal journey made it more and more difficult to involve himself with a church community. Some years later, he studied psychology and found psychoanalytic theories about the roots of religious behaviour very persuasive. 'I no longer pray,' he said at that point. 'I realised I had been petitioning my super-ego for years.' In spite of that remark, although he has not been to church for some time, he has not abandoned Christian belief. It would perhaps be fairer to say he no longer knows what to do with it, and this is a matter of great sadness for him. 'I would like to be a Christian by myself,' he said. 'Technically I can, but in practice, no. I feel less of a Christian for not going to church.' At work he is sometimes asked by colleagues if he is a Christian. 'Ten years ago I would have said yes.' Two years ago, however, he was asked, 'You are not religious are you?', and replied, 'Well, not like that.' The problem, as far as Jeffrey is concerned, is not with what he believes so much as with finding that expressed in church. Associated with this is the difficulty of what it would mean to identify himself to colleagues as a Christian: 'I'm more inclined now, when asked if I am religious, to say, "Tell me what you mean." I've become increasingly sensitive to what the question might mean to the questioner. But it takes an awful lot of time and energy to qualify your answer.'

Events in a person's life: Celia's story (2)

There are countless instances of people who have been sustained through disasters in their lives by the ministry of the church in sacrament and pastoral care. Here, however, we will pick up Celia's story at a point when those structures were unable to provide for her to face the truth of her own life. This part of the story involves two priests, whom we will call Father X and Father Y. For our purposes, Father X represents the 'Come follow me and take up your cross' aspect of Christ's call: he is an Anglo-Catholic traditionalist, with a strong sense of duty. Father Y appears to be more in the 'Come unto me' mode. Also an Anglo-Catholic priest, he is nevertheless a product of the Enlightenment and at the time of Celia's personal trial is even training as a psychotherapist.

In Chapter 2 we followed Celia's journey into the church, and we resume her story in the early 1960s, when she is married, with four children. The whole family went to church together, along with her mother-in-law who was a committed church member. Celia herself became very devout, finding the framework of services, sacraments and the liturgical cycle extremely sustaining and helpful. The event that toppled this structure was that it became obvious that her husband suffered from mental health problems, and her marriage started to go badly wrong. In some ways it is an extreme story – and we should be grateful to her for her courage in sharing it – but it brings together many elements that are by no means unusual in church life, and what happened will be familiar to a great many churchgoers, as well as to pastors and counsellors.

During this period, Celia went regularly to confession to Father X, the parish priest. She spoke of the difficulties in her married life and was told that this was the cross she had to bear and that it was her job to make things as easy as possible for her husband. At the same time, Father X suggested that she seek Marriage Guidance counselling. Quite reasonably, the counsellor said that she could only work with the marriage if both parties would come. Celia's husband not only refused when she suggested this to him, but 'I got severely beaten up – these assaults were becoming more frequent now.'

Celia had sincerely taken up the call to follow Christ in cross-bearing, but the situation in which she now was generated painful internal conflict. It was not simply that she knew what she *should* do and did not want to do it. She wanted the marriage to survive, but by treating it as a cross she had to bear she found herself in a false situation: 'I had religious reasons for wanting the marriage to survive, but at the same time it seemed to me that I was colluding in a tremendous lie. We appeared outwardly as a loving, churchgoing and devoted family, yet at home life had become grotesque and unreal.' To make matters even more complicated, her husband then expressed a vocation to ordination, and with the help of the parish clergy and archdeacon, the practical processes towards this began. Given the way things were at home it must have been hard for Celia to imagine how she would function as his wife when he was ordained. Nevertheless, she continued to struggle under the weight of the cross she was carrying and to try to access its redemptive qualities. 'During that Lent', she said, 'my "special intention" was for his vocation and for an increase of love for him in myself.' She had been taught by Father X that to say you loved a person helped you to love them: 'I believed that and worked hard towards it.'

All the same, her husband's mental state deteriorated steadily. Father Y, who was a friend, recognised that there were problems and was able to persuade him to seek help. Even so, there came a night when Celia was so seriously assaulted by her husband that she ended up in hospital. He was sectioned as an alternative to a prison sentence. The hospital doctors recommended that there should be an injunction to prevent him coming to the house, but a solicitor she consulted had little faith in the effectiveness of this, and recommended divorce. Celia's personal conflict deepened, and at first she resisted this idea: 'I had been confirmed in the Anglo-Catholic tradition and knew that the church would not be happy with this.' The two priests had different attitudes to the situation. When she asked the advice of Father X (her confessor), 'he said that marriage vows stipulated "in sickness and in health" and that if I did instigate divorce proceedings he would bar me from communion'. Father Y thought this unreasonable: even the Roman Catholic Church, he said, would allow her an annulment in these circumstances. Celia's own gut reaction was that 'pair-bonding was for life – but we had never bonded'. She told Father X that she had decided on divorce, and 'he said he did not expect to see me in church again'.

There followed a period of great isolation and bewilderment in which Celia was cut off from the church community as well as from her mother-in-law. Father X, quite rightly, continued to visit and support her husband, who was still a church member. Though we may find his treatment of Celia harsh, he followed through his duty when it came to caring for her husband, and perhaps he considered him, being ill and in psychiatric hospital, as in greater need. Meanwhile Father Y supported Celia, though as a friend, since he was not her parish priest. It could be said that Father X's boundaries were too tightly drawn: it turned out that Father Y's were far from adequate. To put it another way, Father X relied too much on the external structures, and was unable to see past them; Father Y hoped to transcend them, but his own internal structures were not strong enough. His feelings for Celia were mightier than the structure of his priestly identity. It soon transpired that his own marriage was unhappy and he began to talk about himself getting a divorce and marrying Celia – altogether more than she was able – or, indeed willing! – to take on board at the time. He became increasingly importunate and persistent, and she brought the relationship to an end.

Eventually, with the help of work colleagues, Celia managed to buy a house for herself and the children: the day they moved in 'was one of the happiest days of my life and I still feel the same about it more than forty years later.' She grew more and more convinced that the time had come 'to stand on my own two feet without church or clergy', and that 'was what I did for the next few years'. 'I felt distinctly "off" the church and "off" the clergy in particular.' It may be surprising to some that this was not the end of Celia's relationship with church, however, and we will return to her story at a later point.

Christ's crucifixion: the supreme example

The supreme example, of course, of the event being mightier than the structure is the crucifixion. At that point, even the Apostles had not yet understood what Jesus had been telling them. The project was over, and the sense of failure and betrayal must have been overwhelming. Thomas' reaction to being told of the resurrection speaks volumes about the level of disappointment he experienced – it would simply be too painful to raise unreal hopes: 'Unless I see in his hands the print of the nails, and place my finger in the mark of the nails, and place my hand in his side, I will not believe' (John 20:24). And he was not alone in this. When the women first took the news of the resurrection to the Apostles, they dismissed what they had to say as 'an idle tale, and they did not believe them' (Luke 24:12). There are several occasions on which disciples recognise the resurrected Christ, but dare not name the thought, for example on the road to Emmaus (Luke 24), or when he meets a group of them on the shores of the Sea of Tiberias, when 'none of the disciples dared ask him, "Who are you?" They knew it was the Lord' (John 29:12).

When, for whatever reason, our sense of church is shattered, as the crucifixion shattered the hopes of the Apostles, we have few options. Judas, overcome by guilt, despaired and killed himself.

The other Apostles ran away and hid. The women behaved as women always had and took spices to anoint the body. All of them believed that Jesus was dead, and even after the resurrection, it took time to take in that he was alive. Elements of all these reactions are present in our responses to catastrophe in church life. It can seem that we have reached the end of the road. We can compartmentalise church from the rest of our lives – hiding from ourselves; or we can exclude ourselves – hiding from the church.

Reaching the end of the road

'It is not that Judas didn't love Jesus,' someone once said to me, 'he couldn't stand the waiting.' Regardless of its accuracy, this is a very interesting interpretation of the betrayal of Christ. It implies that for Judas to do what he did, he must have invested great personal hope in Jesus as the Messiah, and become mortally discouraged by the way things were going. Both Matthew and Mark describe Judas as going to bargain with the authorities immediately after the incident of the woman who anointed Christ's feet with precious ointment (Matthew 26; Mark 14). We are also told (John 13:29) that Judas kept the money box for the group: it was he who would be sent out to buy food, or to distribute money to the poor. Both Matthew and Mark tell us that some people were outraged by what they saw as the waste of the ointment, which could have been sold for a large sum to give to the poor. Jesus speaks out in support of the woman; marvellous though that is, it is not our concern here.

If Judas was already beginning to doubt that Jesus was the Messiah, this incident of the anointing would be just the kind of thing to trigger his despair of Jesus ever fulfilling his destiny. With hindsight, we can see these events leading up not only to the crucifixion but also the resurrection. But Luke also tells us (22:3) that Satan – the father of lies – entered into Judas: Satan, that great whisperer of destructive ideas, the stirrer of discontent ('God knows that if you eat of it your eyes will be opened, and you will be like God ...').

When something in which we have invested a great deal of hope begins to crumble, and we are in pain, it is difficult not to become destructive, simply because the pain itself is unbearable, and we begin to feel that it must come to an end, whatever else needs to come to an end in order for that to happen. For example, when caring for a dying person, however much we love them, we may long for the suffering – theirs and ours – to be over so much that signs of recovery may become as painful as signs of deterioration. Similarly, in a situation where someone or something we believe in appears to be failing, it can also be so painful that we want to destroy our own hope: we look for signs that they were not worth believing in in the first place. In this frame of mind it would be easy to hear Christ's defence of the woman as mere inflation: 'Why do you trouble this woman? For she has done a beautiful thing to me. For you always have the poor with you, but you will not always have me. In pouring this ointment on my body she has done it to prepare me for burial. Truly, I say to you, wherever this gospel is preached in the whole world, what she has done will be told in memory of her' (Matthew 26:10–13).

All this is said not to defend Judas, but to illustrate that just as we can only really be betrayed by a trusted friend (the damage done by an 'open enemy' is bearable in a way that damage inflicted by a friend is not),[2] the greater the hope we invest in the church the greater the sense of despair we may feel when things go badly wrong. A man who had given his life to the church as a priest and teacher, and had survived no end of difficulties in various church communities, found himself almost terminally discouraged by a trivial incident, where the generous offer of a friend to help a group of people out of a difficult situation was rejected for petty reasons. He knew the context was trivial, but to him it spoke of the whole mess of humanity – the escalation of violence, the destruction of the planet, and, above all, what seemed like a complete failure of the message which had sustained his life. He found himself praying to God to accept that he (God) had failed, and to bring the whole thing – the world, the creation, the human race – to an end. Like Ivan Karamazov, he had reached a point where the scale of suffering was not worth redemption. He wanted to 'return the ticket'.[3] If these were the terms on which eternal life was offered, oblivion would be preferable.

This man was sensible enough – and fortunate enough – to gather around him a group of friends who were able to act as a church for him. They were not all members of his own church, but they were all believers in the Christian story. They were able to acknowledge the good reasons for his despair, but also draw on their communal hope, and he found the courage to go on. The structure held – but so often it does not. As one woman put it: 'In the church there is no affirmation, no sharing, no levelling. There are only people who always *seem* to be all right, and the clergy are running around manically and unavailable. Yet we are all needy. There is such a need for mutual support.'

Hiding from ourselves – compartmentalisation

A nurse with many years' experience once described to me how, whenever she went into a bank, she suddenly felt about three years old. It was a context where she had no skill, and her adult experience deserted her. We can often see the same kind of thing happening when people go into churches. I have long maintained that one reason church choirs are such hotbeds of rivalry and discontent is that for many people who join them the last time they sang in a choir was in adolescence. It is therefore their adolescent selves they bring to the church choir, not the mature adults they are in other respects.

Some years ago, the American psychologist Anna-Maria Rizutto interviewed people about their family histories and their understanding of God. One of her conclusions was that there is no need to teach children to believe in God. This comes to them naturally. What they learn about God, however, is a different matter. This learning comes from direct teaching, but more especially from the ways in which parents and other people behave towards them and each other. It is in this experience of growing up that our natural propensity to believe in God is filled out by an individual understanding. 'No six year old', says Rizutto, 'comes to church without his own pet God under his arm.'[4] This may be true of 16- and 60-year-olds too – that God is composed of memories, experiences, parental assumptions. Whether we are lifelong churchgoers, or take it up or return to it later in life, walking into church can take us directly back to childhood patterns of thinking and understanding which need to catch up with our other adult abilities. A middle-aged woman who had brought up her own family and held down a responsible job confided that she had never been able to let go of church altogether. 'I say the "Our Father" every night before I go to bed,' she said. 'That way I am covered if there is a God and I have not lost anything if there isn't.' It goes without saying that if she had applied this level of thinking to the rest of her life, she would hardly have survived.

The character Helen Reed in David Lodge's novel *Thinks* provides a clear and typical account of this childish (as opposed to child-like) approach to religion.[5] After she left the church as an undergraduate, church became the place for getting married, baptising children, attending midnight Mass at Christmas 'with my parents for old times' sake'. When her husband dies, however, Helen makes tentative forays into church, 'out of a confused jumble of motives. Perhaps I feared superstitiously that the Catholic God had punished me for my apostasy, and that I'd better get back on good terms with Him before He did something else terrible to me or my children.'

This regression in the face of religion brings both problems and advantages. It means we see some things more clearly than we otherwise would, and others less so. It is an opportunity to 'become as little children', and at the same time can leave us disorientated, unable to match what we find with our adult experience. A highly skilled and experienced therapist, who also happens to be a clergy daughter, described her feelings on going into a cathedral. 'Such a glorious building,' she said, 'but it is full of women with those robes, and things round their necks, and they look down their nose at you and make you feel like a little slug. I can't stand it – I absolutely can't stand it because I know that in the eyes of anyone to do with the church I am a sinner and that's that.' Being the kind of person she was, she heard herself at that point and added, with a laugh, 'That's not disconnected with being brought up in the church, is it.'

Compartmentalisation does not only, of course, take place between adult and child, but between different aspects of our adult selves. There are many ardent workers for the church who live in an almost Jekyll and Hyde way: they care for their parishioners and neglect or even abuse their wives and children; they may be charismatic leaders of prayer but their personal and sexual lives are in utter chaos; they impose church discipline on others without observing it themselves. 'I was barred for communion for years because I was in a gay relationship,' a man said. 'I accepted it as the normal discipline of the church. Then the priest who had been my confessor was arrested for cottaging. I accept the church is hypocritical, but this really was taking things a bit far.' Another man – a charismatic priest – described to me how he needed the rules of the church to keep him on the straight and narrow, but also to be able to experience himself as both a good person and a bad person. As well as keeping the rules, he also needed them in order, from time to time, to break them.

Hiding from the church

One way in which the event can be mightier than the structure is an occasion – or even a choice – in one's own life that appears to make it simply impossible to continue to belong. 'I was seventeen when I fell in love for the first time,' said Sarah, now in her fifties, 'and it was with a woman. I didn't even bother to ask whether I could go on being part of the church as a lesbian. I just assumed that was it. In any case, thinking of my church community then I don't know who I could have asked. I remember going through a massive conflict about it because it wasn't just church – I seriously believed I would burn in hell if I followed my feelings. But I also believed it was worth it. I suppose it was a sort of Faustian bargain. Years later a priest told me I had been absolutely right – which seemed very enlightened and helpful until I realised he meant it in the sense that I was right in thinking I could have my lover or the church, not both. I had never even heard of the LGCM [Lesbian and Gay Christian Movement]. When I did finally realise that there were people who insisted on bringing their whole gay selves into church I was overwhelmed. It seemed so courageous, and so marvellous, and I just wished I had come across them sooner.'

Where do we go from here?

Unless, like George, we encounter clear-cut doctrinal reasons that indicate a change of church, on the whole moving from one church to another is liable merely to transfer the problem: there seems ultimately little to choose between one church and another, so we have to make up our minds whether to leave or stay. The next part of our trial concerns what the church is actually for.

7

What is it all for?

Question: What is the difference between church and football?
Answer: You don't need to buy a ticket to go to church.

At a seminar on ritual an ordinand gave a convincing presentation in which he demonstrated that there was little difference between a football match and a Sunday service. People came together, they wore special clothes – he pointed out the similarities between a stole and a scarf – and shared deeply in a common experience. Similar analogies can, of course, be made with common meals, with music-making – in fact with almost anything people do together. From an Orthodox point of view this apparent relativisation of church activity is absolutely correct. Although the church is responsible for the particular sacraments (communion, confession, marriage, baptism, etc.), ultimately anything can be a sacrament – anything, that is, that facilitates the inbreaking of the Spirit into the world. This is not to say that the work of the church in this regard is unnecessary: rather that it is a special – and important – case of God's activity among us.

If, however, we have many and varied ways of relating to God and each other outside the church, what is the church itself for? Is it necessary, or would football or some other activity do as well? A meditation group would, perhaps, be a more obvious substitute than football, and I asked Alice, a Roman Catholic who goes to a weekly meditation group, to compare this group with her church. There are similarities: both meet weekly, and both involve a degree of habit, expectation and effort. Both provide a common mystical experience. In the meditation group – rather more than the church community – Alice is confident they could all call on each other in a time of trouble. Unlike the church, the meditation group rejects the idea of embracing any particular teaching. People – as she believes people always will – come together to make their own community, and this in turn provides social support. On that level, church as such is unnecessary.

On another level, however, Alice is convinced that the church, though it is less successful than the meditation group in providing a shared mystical experience, is nevertheless important. Unlike the group, it stands for a traditional practice of the Christian faith, and also for symbolism, pattern and continuity: 'the impersonal pageant of ritual'. For Alice, then, the essential function of the church is twofold: to keep the Eucharist going, because this is what was initiated by Christ, and to preserve and keep the Gospel.

Do Christians need the church?

It may be that the primary role of the church lies in maintaining the Christian tradition, in both practice and teaching. A key question, however, is whether, in order to define oneself as a Christian, it is necessary to belong to a church. Whatever theologians or the churches themselves may have to say about this, people on the ground have a number of different views.

John – not surprisingly, perhaps, for a lawyer – thinks the question can be answered both positively and negatively. His 'yes' is that, in practice, interaction with others is necessary to provide the material that gets you to the point of becoming a Christian, and it is important for people to join together for worship, Bible reading and so on. Like Alice, then, he sees the church as having an essential role in preserving the Gospel. It could be said, he added, that one was not fully Christian unless one was part of a church. On the other hand, he said, being a Christian is about the relationship between God and oneself. John became a Christian through an understanding of himself and God, and the need for his own acceptance of himself, 'and this in no way required a church community'. At a mystical level, John's experience is essentially solitary: 'The Eucharist', he said, 'is a service I enjoy – it is multi-layered – but it is about my receiving the bread and wine and how I respond. I have no sense of corporate belonging from it as other people seem to. The moments at which I am trying to connect with God are moments when I shut out the rest of the world.' At the same time there is a clear distinction for him between this very private experience and trying to put the Christian faith into practice: 'The times when I am trying to live out the Christian faith, or see someone else do so, are of a very different kind from the private moments when I commune with God. They don't overlap. They are different kinds of experience.'

For some people the issue simply does not arise: 'My parents would describe themselves as Christians,' said one person, 'though they have never been churchgoers.' Anna, who had been a churchgoer in her early teens, and again as a young adult, said it never occurred to her to seek out a new church when she moved house in her late twenties, although she had found the previous one a good experience: 'I liked the music and the discussion groups were good. The discussions were on issues to do with living rather than about God. But no, I don't think one church has anything to do with any other, so I didn't think to look for a new one. I believe in God, but that has not got anything to do with churchgoing.'

'It depends on your definition of a Christian,' said Liz, an Anglican priest: 'At theological college what you are trained to say, when the inevitable Baptism family come along and say, "We don't go to church vicar, but we *are* Christians", is, "Well, one of Jesus' last commandments to us was 'Do this in remembrance of me.'" But actually I think that wears a bit thin, because of course he didn't say, "Gather together once a week in large outdated buildings and have a very ritualised version of a meal." He said, "Meet together, share food, share drink, talk about me, think about me, remember me – and try to remember some of the things I have taught you." So no, I don't think you do have to go to church to be a Christian.' Asked what she thought Jesus meant, then, when he said to Peter 'On this rock I will build my church', she replied, 'Church at the time was really house church, wasn't it. Who knows? Maybe he meant go home and start a lay group. *I* don't know what he meant.' The way Liz thinks about these things has no effect on her commitment to the priesthood: she simply refuses to insist that the churches' way of being Christian is the only one.

A similar view is taken by Michael, who, as we saw in Chapter 4, felt deeply betrayed by the church, and who works with people who are seriously ill and dying: 'I have a life in that [the Christian] story. The God I relate to is a Christian one – but I certainly would not say I belong to a church. It means that a lot of people assume I have no beliefs, which is personally quite hard – but it is important since it enables a lot of conversations to take place.'

Alan, a church organist, also feels that belief in the Christian story does not necessarily imply going to church. As he thought about it further, however, he began to uncover doubts about his own answer, since the Gospel is so deeply concerned with how we relate to others. 'It is the duty of Christians to engage with other Christians,' he went on, 'and it would be very odd if that did not happen at least partly in a liturgical context. It is not an absolute commitment – but it is inconceivable that it wouldn't happen.' For Alan it is important that people – unless they have a specific vocation to the solitary life – come together to worship because belief is not something that takes place in a vacuum. 'If you are going to have spiritual beliefs,' he said, 'you have to expose yourself to other people's understanding of them.' He could imagine living a very moral life and having a private spirituality – 'but I cannot imagine what kind of spirituality you would have that you want to keep it hidden. It would theoretically be possible to live in the most ethical way and privately be spiritual – but it is hard to imagine why one would wish to do that or what kind of spirituality you would have. I see genuine spirituality as being communal in its very essence.' For Alan, then, spirituality itself has a communal dimension – which for Christians presumably points towards the church. His partner, however, a lay pastoral assistant in a busy Anglican church, was not so sure: 'You can be Christian without the church,' she said. 'The communal aspect is more fulfilling, but it is not essential. It magnifies the gift.'

This is, of course, a very interesting statement, implying that the church opens out our spiritual experience, although in her view this is not necessary in order to practise the faith. In these terms, church membership is a choice, and it does indeed place the church on trial. What do you do if you find it is shrinking rather than magnifying the gift, as was the experience of a woman – a believer – who described church as 'a Christian prison which makes me less of a Christian'?

The question of how church relates to belief is extremely complex. When Frances left the Anglican Church in early adulthood, this meant she had ceased to believe, but this did not necessarily operate the other way round. When, through contact with sisters at the local Catholic convent and through Orthodox worship, she rediscovered a relationship with Christ, she did not see church membership as a natural consequence: 'Christ was my life. Church did not have to be.' It was other people, rather than Frances herself, who thought it was essential for her to become a member of the church, and having left, as we saw in the previous chapter, her belief in the Christian story and her desire to participate in communal worship remained intact.

There are those for whom Christianity and church are inseparable. Claire, for example, was quite definite that they belong together. 'They can't not,' she said, 'I don't know what that would mean. People say, "I am a spiritual person but church doesn't do anything for me" – but you have to have a community identity. You do have to meet together and name what you believe. Muslims understand this very well.'

The 'full beauty of the incarnation'

What *do* Christians believe? I was asked this recently by a friend who comes occasionally to my church. I thought about it and replied, 'I suppose we believe what is summarised in the Creed.' She went away and reported what I had said to another friend of hers who is also a regular churchgoer. The next time we met she said, 'I mentioned to So-and-so what you said about the Creed, and she was very surprised. She said "Nobody bothers with that any more." ' This was fascinating, because for me the recitation of the Creed in the liturgy is an ongoing challenge: do I believe this? What does it mean if I do? And it is perhaps worth spending a little time on its central claim: that God became human.

Christianity teaches a personal God who is not only the source of all being, but who entered history, coming into the world at a particular time as a particular person: Jesus Christ. What Jeffrey refers to as 'the full beauty of the incarnation', and what he so desperately wants the church to preach, is that Jesus is not just a divinely inspired man, nor is he a super-hero who saves the world by being God. He is not even a 50/50 mixture of these two, but 100 per cent human *and* 100 per cent God. This is, and always has been, very hard for Christians – or anyone else – to get their heads round, and it took the church itself nearly half a millennium to formulate it. Various attempts to understand the incarnation – otherwise known as heresies – were finally set aside at the Council of Chalcedon in 451, where five hundred bishops managed to find an agreed formula to express the mystery of the person of Christ:

> *We all with one voice confess our Lord Jesus Christ one and the same Son, the same perfect in Godhead, the same perfect in manhood, truly God and truly man ... of one substance with the Father as touching the Godhead, the same of one substance with us as touching the manhood ... to be acknowledged in two natures, without confusion, without change, without division, without separation; the distinction of natures being in no way abolished because of the union.*[1]

We can, perhaps, express something of this formula visually as follows (Table 1):

Table 1: The Body of Christ (1)

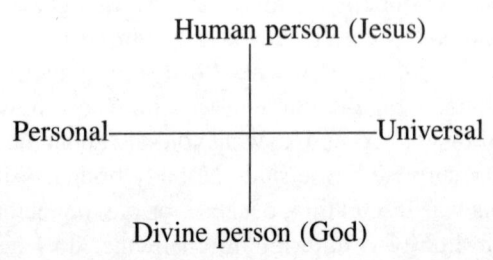

```
                Human person (Jesus)
                         |
    Personal ────────────┼──────────── Universal
                         |
                 Divine person (God)
```

The vertical axis expresses the two natures of the incarnate Christ as both fully human and fully divine. The horizontal axis expresses the personal and universal aspects of God's relationship with the world. The word 'universal' implies not only everyone living, but all those who have ever lived, and the cosmos itself. The axes themselves operate on a 'both–and' rather than an 'either–or' basis. Christ does not cease to be God in order to be human; nor does he cease to be human when he returns to the Godhead. Neither does any person's relationship with Christ happen in isolation: it is both unique to that person and part of the whole connectedness of the human race, alive and dead, and ultimately part of our relationship with nature itself.

At a cosmic level, Christ is also the *Logos*, the eternal Word, and the deep structure of all created things. His incarnation as a human being is a particular revelation to us, but God is revealed in the whole natural world, and when we pray we are taking part in an ongoing hymn of praise and thanksgiving offered to the Creator by all that is created: by the natural world which is accessible to our physical senses, and by the unseen world (angels, archangels, powers, etc.) that is not. Whether we take part in it or not, this is something that goes on all the time:

> *All the spiritual powers tremble before thee. The sun sings thy praises; the moon glorifies thee; the stars supplicate before thee; the light obeys thee; the deeps are afraid at thy presence; the fountains are thy servants ... the angelic powers minister to thee, the choirs of archangels worship thee; the many-eyed cherubim and six-winged seraphim, standing round thee and flying about thee, hide their faces in fear of thine unapproachable glory ...*[2]

This, of course, is a marvellous piece of poetry. Before going any further, however, it is important to make clear that by talking of the cosmic liturgy in this way, and of God being revealed in nature, we are not subscribing to the way in which the churches use so-called arguments from 'natural law' to prescribe how human beings should live. Most of such arguments are based on a very limited understanding of nature, and fall well short of any true scientific observation or approach. There is, however, a level at which we can understand creation as shot through with God's energy, as described by Pamela Vermes in her poem 'The Riddle of the Sparks':

> There was a tap-tap-tapping
> of sparks
> of the one huge sparkle of God
> wishing to come out.
> There was a tapping in big and faraway things
> such as the sky with birds in it
> and the earth with rocks and stones
> and with trees and flowers
> and animals on it.
>
> But there was also a tapping
> in things that are little and near
> such as the pot with a flower in it ...
> They've each got one of their own!
> the people cried.
> And *Without End* said:
> I know I know.
>
> *Without End* was God, you see.[3]

This beautiful poem is inspired by an ancient Jewish mystical account of creation. It demonstrates throughout the extraordinary paradox of a Creator God who also speaks personally with the people he has created, and who is progressively revealed throughout the Old Testament. From a Christian point of view these 'sparks' are in fact the cosmic Christ.

This transcendent God, then, 'uncircumscribed, without beginning and beyond speech',[4] is the very same God who is born as a human being, entering into that unique state in creation where material being, spirit and consciousness meet. He does so to heal the division that has come about between himself and creation, and also to heal the divisions within creation: between its material and spiritual dimensions, between ourselves and the natural world, between ourselves and other people, and indeed between different parts of ourselves. The whole world is fallen, the whole world needs redemption, but as human beings we are uniquely capable of acting in such a way that things are moved in a Godward direction. This is why the early church fathers fiercely resisted the idea of a dualism between matter and spirit: precisely because it is only as being both material beings made from the earth (*humus*) and at the same time spiritual beings drawn towards God that we can act as the essential bridge between God and a fallen world. This is the priestly calling of all human beings. Christ, the great High Priest, 'neither angel nor ambassador but the Lord himself made flesh',[5] is the unique, perfect instance, but each one of us is also in that high priestly position, and so is the church itself, as the Body of Christ.

The church as the Body of Christ

As the continuing Body of Christ the church, then, embraces both human and divine, both immanent and transcendent, both individual and social – and indeed the whole created universe. It expresses the personal relationship of a loving God with each and every one of us, and also the way in which that love connects us to each other. It is incarnational, bringing God's love to birth in this world, and it is mystical, existing also in the unseen world, taking part in the cosmic liturgy of all creation, seen and unseen.

The incarnational church is involved in teaching and preaching, witness, social and political action, pastoral care. As we have seen, when the church is functioning well in people's lives, all these things form part of its life in this world. As one priest put it, the church's witness is – or should be – primarily a question of demonstrating that anyone is welcome and can be included. God – and the church – are for everyone. She referred to Ghandi's remark, when he was asked why he was not a Christian: 'I don't reject your Christ. I love your Christ. It's just that so many of you Christians are so unlike your Christ.' This, she thought, should resonate with all Christians: church communities should strive to be 'a haven of kindness'. For her, the church is 'an attempt to make manifest the love and glory of God in the world'. It is 'not just a cult, or social support, or a set of rules – it is real, it is about God who will love you into wholeness'.

The mystical church is expressed in individual and corporate prayer. At best, church should be the proper channel for the spiritual life. As Michael put it, 'This is something human we need to do, and church is one way of addressing it. Without church there is no cap to the volcano, and society is in trouble. It needs to be there for the people who can't blaze their own trail. Without it, people simply try and re-invent their own rituals.' What is unique about Christianity is the radical claim of incarnation: God, the divine person, lives among us as a human person. The church itself is not just a gateway to the transcendent but is that living personal body.

The church, then, brings together all these aspects of human personhood in relation to God. It is – in essence if not in practice – the place where each one of us is most truly ourselves, and where we are at the same time most connected. It takes up the work of the incarnate Christ, doing the Father's will, existing to teach people about God through preaching and also through action – by healing, by protesting against injustice, by witnessing to God's love. At the same time it is an image of Christ as one of the persons of the Trinity, invoking the Spirit, praying to the Father – expressing our deep personal unity with each other and with God.

A eucharistic understanding of the church

As creation offering itself back to the Creator, it could be said that potentially the whole world, the whole cosmos, is church, but at a level which is inaccessible to any ordinary human experience. The church embraces everything on such a vast scale that no one of us – not even any group of us – will be able to encompass it all. Our participation in any aspect of the life of the church is necessarily partial, as is (*pace* claims by various bodies to be 'the one true church') that of any church. And of course, any of the functions that church fulfils can carry on whether people define themselves as church or not. People will always pray, will always exercise compassion, stand out against injustice, gather together for rites of passage and so on, whether the churches as we know them today survive or not.

How people perceive the function of the church, and how they enter into its life, will vary according to their particular experiences, needs and natural tendencies. One thing the church does, however, by embracing all these aspects of the incarnate God, is to provide a place where all these things converge, in the Eucharist. The Eucharist is incarnational: it uses bread and wine, it is celebrated by human beings, it commemorates actual events in history. It is also mystical, offering to God what God has given, and participating here and now in the self-giving of Christ, and in the Kingdom to come. We can, then, 'map' the Body of Christ with Eucharist at its centre as follows (Table 2):

Table 2: The Body of Christ (2)

	Immanent	
	Spiritual guidance, pastoral care, personal life and relationships	Political action, community, teaching, preaching, witness
Individual	————EUCHARIST————	Social
	Prayer, mysticism, repentance, vigilance of soul	Shared worship, ritual, communion of saints, participation in life of Christ
	Transcendent	

Participation in the Eucharist, as we have seen, can be a deeply personal experience. It is where we find ourselves, in the gift of bread and wine, loved by God, and can experience this relationship at its most individual. The Eucharist is not only the place where the personal, the social, the immanent and the transcendent converge, but a place they can pass through and become mingled with each other. It is the place where the Body is broken in order that 'we being many' may be 'one body, for we all partake of the one bread' – the place of unity. By taking part, we can experience something of that deep connection, with people all over the world and throughout the centuries, and with the unseen, immaterial world as well.

There is no doubt that experiences that take place within the Eucharist are beyond rational analysis. Anyone who is part of leading or organising worship, as priest, choir member, steward, for example, will be aware of the way in which it can be celebrated in situations of extreme tension among the immediate participants

– 'Small village, big hell', as the Argentineans say – and yet the service itself transcends all of that and is experienced as particularly peaceful by people present. It dissipates emotion and enables us to forget ourselves, if only for a few moments. The Eucharist binds the individual with the social body in ways that are not immediately obvious, but which bring about internal change in the participants. An Anglican priest described the communion rail as both horizontal and vertical: 'It is a personal relationship with God, but you are also alongside other people. You can't ignore it for long, if you go all the time and mean it.'

On the right-hand side of our 'map', we can see that even in our partial – *intra*-church – unity, the Eucharist connects us, or, rather incarnates our connection, with people around the world at a practical level. Mary, a Catholic, said, 'I can go anywhere in the world, in any language, and I can go to a Catholic church and follow the Mass. The structure is the same, I know where I am and I can participate.'

As the Body of Christ, however, the whole church already exists in complete oneness: its unity is, in fact, at a deep level, unbroken. In its incarnate form – us – we cannot yet experience that except as described by a man who talked about the prayer for the peace of the church that takes place after the 'Our Father' in the Roman Mass: 'I used to think of that as a prayer for Christian unity – for the unification of all Christians, asking for something that doesn't exist. But when we use it in the Mass I realise that it is about preserving what *does* exist – it is given to us by Christ.'

Any Eucharist we celebrate will only partially express our oneness with each other, and indeed with the whole of creation, because in the world we inhabit the body is fragmented, and it will continue to be so until the end of time. As John put it, the lack of unity between the churches has to be understood as an outcome of human nature, it belongs in the upper half of our map. 'It is simply not possible for us all to live together under one set of rules and traditions,' he said. 'To expect that would be to expect us to be Christ-like.'

At the same time any Eucharist we celebrate participates in the ongoing outpouring of God's love to creation and the thanksgiving offered in return to God. It is in the Eucharist that we find the tension between the now and the yet to come in which the church properly lives: like each human being, it is fully present in time and space, and at the same time concerned with the imperceptible world that is drawing us towards our ultimate fulfilment *beyond* time and space. John went on to make a very important point: 'Of course, we *should* be Christ-like,' he added, 'but we also have to be practical. It is unrealistic to expect us to be unified – if we could be, we would not need Christ.'

8

The body broken

> I would like to see communion become true communion – for all the churches to be able to receive communion together. I would like to take you [Orthodox] and my husband [Anglican] to my church [Roman Catholic].
> I receive in the Anglican church occasionally – I have a huge crisis of faith every time I do it – but I feel I must do it at least once a year because it is my husband's church, and we go together each week.

Only by being broken can the body be shared. In the Orthodox liturgy leavened bread is used and before the Eucharist, the celebrant carves out a central piece – the lamb – from the loaf. It is this piece that is eventually broken up and mingled in the chalice with the wine and given in communion. These preparations generally take place in the sanctuary, and the sanctuary is usually invisible because of an icon screen between it and the main body of the church: we do not see the cutting of the loaf. It can, then, be a freshly startling experience to be at a Eucharist in a Western church where everything is visible, and where the altar is placed so that everyone can see what is going on. At an Anglican Eucharist I attended recently, unleavened wafers were used, and I was powerfully struck by the drama of the moment when the priest, facing us, lifted the large host up and, breaking it, said, 'This is my body broken for you.' The perfect white circle in his hands snapped in two with a resounding crack: 'My body, broken for you.'

This – the sharing of the broken body – is the focus of our unity. Yet I was not able to receive communion at that Eucharist (because of the strictures of my own church, not theirs), although I was able to participate completely in the service in every other way. The fact that we cannot all receive communion together means that *the focus of our unity is also the point at which we most deeply experience our divisions*. This happens both at the level of what goes on between the church and the individual, and in what goes on between churches.

The body withheld

Both the Orthodox and Roman Catholic Churches keep careful boundaries around communion, though they are not necessarily the same, and many clergy themselves struggle to make sense of the rules in the light of how they understand the Gospel. There is a story of a young Catholic priest who goes to see an old mentor of his, and describes how a divorced woman came to him for communion during the Mass. 'And what did you do?' asks the old priest. The young man hesitates, and then says earnestly, 'I did what I thought Christ would have done.' The older man recoils in horror. 'You didn't, did you!' More often, however, it is as one woman described it: 'It's terrible. I go to church and there are all these sad people at the back who cannot go to communion because they are divorced or have married someone who is divorced and they will only receive communion on their deathbed.'

Precisely because participation in the Eucharist through communion is experienced as healing, exclusion for whatever reason is a very painful matter. It is easy to assume that people who have left the church or have made choices that exclude them from communion do not care very much about communion, but this is far from the truth. An army wife talked about a Mass celebrated on an isolated army base by a Roman Catholic priest. Since all the women had collaborated in decorating the chapel he used a special dispensation to allow the Protestant women to come to communion. This dispensation did not, however, extend to the Catholic wives of men who had previously been divorced, one of whom was standing next to the woman who told me this story: 'She stood there with tears streaming down her face.'

Many people, like the young priest in the Catholic joke, find it difficult to reconcile personal exclusion from communion with an understanding of a Gospel of love. In practice, people can find themselves subject to church disciplines around communion which seem to cling on to arbitrary laws with no regard as to what it means for one person to love another.

It is perhaps a relatively straightforward matter for someone who is being unfaithful in a marriage to be refused communion, but there are many situations that people find it difficult to understand. For example, an Orthodox woman – a widow – was told by her confessor not to go to communion because she was having a sexual relationship with a man to whom she was not married. As a twenty-first-century adult woman she could not see anything morally wrong with this relationship between two otherwise unattached adults who were both past childbearing age, and who were not certain they wanted to make a commitment to marriage. Furthermore, as a person in society she could not see that her relationship was in any way damaging to anyone. She continued to go to church and experienced not going to communion as extremely painful. Not only did it make her feel 'unclean', and very distressed, but inevitably it coloured her feelings about the relationship itself.

It is now at least theoretically possible for a divorced Catholic who does not engage in a sexual relationship with anyone else to be admitted to communion, but this appears to be by no means automatic, and there is a great deal of painful confusion surrounding this issue, not only in the Catholic Church but more widely. We have seen how as recently as the 1960s Celia, an Anglo-Catholic, was told not even to come to church when she decided divorce was the only way forward, and there are many people who have been – and still find themselves – excluded from communion simply because they are divorced. 'I didn't want a divorce,' said one Catholic woman, 'nor did my sister or my nieces, but they were being beaten up by their husbands. No one *wants* to be divorced.' In order that people should not, as a result of divorce, be excluded from communion for life, this situation often leads to the annulment of what in any ordinary terms – and indeed in legal terms – have been marriages, even if they were disastrous marriages.

Mary, whose marriage was annulled when her daughter was already in her teens, continues to be distressed by how this affected her daughter, who had been raised a Catholic, and who was taking classes to prepare for confirmation at the time of the annulment. 'Seventeen years later,' said Mary, 'she is still telling me what that woman [the catechist] told her: that if your parents' marriage is annulled you become a bastard. I tell her that her parents were legally married and that is why there was a legal divorce – but she still believes to this day that she is a bastard. It is absolutely heartbreaking and very difficult to deal with.' This is not an uncommon story, and has huge implications for the children of such marriages. It is one thing for parents to admit they have not been able to hold together a marriage, and need to divorce, or even that to get married was a terrible mistake – but it is quite another to say they were never married at all.

Mary's daughter did not in the end get confirmed. 'My agreement with her at fifteen was to go to the classes and make a choice, and she went, and decided not.' Now, in her early thirties, she is marrying another non-practising Catholic, and members of the family are very upset they do not intend to marry in church. In order to do so, however, she would not only have to be confirmed, but she would also have to live apart from her fiancé for six months: something that is hardly realistic when they already own their own house together. It is also unrealistic at another level: 'They don't want to do something', said Mary, 'that is not what they are.'

It should be said that priests who exercise these church disciplines are often compassionate and supportive towards the people in the situations that exclude them from communion. 'During my divorce and annulment,' said one woman, 'the [Catholic] church community provided a lot of support. Things were very bad, and I had no money. An envelope would appear in my letterbox with vouchers for Marks and Spencers, or people would give me food. The priest was good, too – very supportive.' When she eventually got remarried – to an Anglican – a Catholic deacon took part in the wedding, and she found this very helpful: 'It meant there was a Catholic aspect to the marriage.'

The problems of communion did not go away, however. Once she had remarried she stopped going to communion in the Roman

Catholic Church – 'I can't tell you how hard that was.' Part of what was so difficult was that she really believed in transubstantiation, which is not an Anglican doctrine. 'It is a core part of my heart and I cannot change that.' She had nevertheless taken communion in the Anglican Church, 'because it's communion – and there is a part of me that says at least once in a while I must take communion'. More often, however, she accompanied her husband to the altar rail but did not receive, because of the fact that he would not be able to come to communion with her in her own church. 'I cross my arms because he can't receive in a Catholic church, though I *can* receive in an Anglican church – and worry about my Catholicism. But it is a heartbreak for him that he cannot receive in my church. We went to Mass once and I went to receive and he sat in the pew and it was heartbreaking – and I thought, "I should not have gone to communion." Communion is supposed to be a union of people – not a division.'

It is also often the case that people exclude themselves from communion, particularly on the basis of Matthew 5:23–24: 'If you are offering your gift at the altar and there remember that your brother has something against you, leave your gift there before the altar and go; first be reconciled to your brother, and then come and offer your gift.' Priests from various churches expressed regret that people allow this to keep them away from communion, seeing it as a misunderstanding, and emphasising the healing effect of regular communion on the communicants. 'People are often told they should not go to communion without going to confession first,' said one Orthodox priest, 'but sometimes you need to go to communion in order to be able to go to confession.' An Anglican priest said that it made her cross when people came to her and said they had not been up to the communion rail to receive because they had had a bad week, 'or hadn't prayed or had been horrible to someone. That', she said 'is when you should be running towards the altar – it's not a smug reward for having done good. People exclude themselves, and we have a duty to make sure people understand that is not the best way to build a relationship with God.'

The body broken – divisions in the wider church

As the focus of our unity, the Eucharist is also the place where divisions in the wider church can be most apparent: where the brokenness of the incarnate social body prevents the sharing of the broken mystical body. The vertical dimension remains intact, each person participating in what is at an ontological level an unbroken unity, but the horizontal social dimension is broken. To many people, both inside and outside the churches, this is simply incomprehensible, as one Catholic woman expressed it: 'Intellectually I understand there are differences in what people believe. I can believe in transubstantiation for example, and others can't – but I don't want them excluded because of that. We do this thing with a group of people in remembrance of Christ – how can we then shut people out?'

Disunity, of course, takes place at every level. Recently, a theologian spent a week at a conference on biblical authority. When I asked her what they discussed, she said they had not got as far as any of the issues on the agenda because the Protestants could not agree with the Orthodox and the Catholics about what constituted the Bible. The Catholics and the Orthodox could not agree which were the fathers of the church and which were heretics – and a Quaker present refused to discuss the early teachers of the church if the Orthodox and Catholics insisted on referring to them all as 'fathers'.

When it comes to communion, Christians are so used to the fact that the Eastern Churches are not in communion with the Western Churches, that Orthodox and Roman Catholics do not recognise Anglican orders, and that the various Eastern Churches are not in communion with each other, we only tend to question it when it affects us personally.

In a world where people did not move around very much, most people would not be personally affected by the disunity of the churches except in times of great ecclesiological change or reform, because there would be only one church serving one particular community – or if there were more than one, most people would tend to be brought up in one or another and, on the whole, stay there. Now, however, with vast movements of people around the world, and massive cultural shifts taking place, the disunity of the churches impinges more and more on people's lives – and when it does, feelings can run very high indeed.

'The church I would not be seen dead in'

There is a story that circulates among the descendants of the Russians of the 'first-wave' emigration – that which followed the 1917 Revolution. A Russian is shipwrecked on a desert island. When he is rescued it is discovered that he built a shelter for himself – and two churches. 'Why two churches?', ask the rescuers. 'Well,' he replies, 'there is one for me to go to – and the one that I would not be seen dead in.' This story reflects the bitterness of divisions that took place among Russian Christians in the West during the Soviet era – a drama that is still being played out in the life of the Orthodox Churches of Western Europe today.

A similar story is told about a marooned Scotsman – except he has three churches: as well as the one he goes to and the one he would not be seen dead in, he also needs one to burn down.

A recent visit to a remote Scottish island was curiously reminiscent of these stories. The island has about fifty inhabitants – around 10 per cent of whom have sought it out as a monastic desert. And, like the Scotsman's desert island, it has three churches: the small church of a tiny Episcopalian community; a beautifully maintained kirk, which has monthly services held by a visiting minister, and a tiny Orthodox chapel. They co-exist, I should say, in harmony. There is, moreover, a history of peaceful co-existence on the island where, by the 1840s, when the population was considerably larger, there were already two churches: Free Kirk and Church of Scotland. A hundred years later, however, many families were going to both, the one in the morning and the other in the evening. Eventually, the Free Kirk building was combined with its hall to make a community centre and the small Church of Scotland church remained. A moving feature of this church was that on the walls, where you would normally expect to see the Stations of the Cross, they had put pictures of children from around the world taken from a UNICEF calendar, and there was a note on the door reminding people to pray for children everywhere as well as the precious children of the island (the school has two pupils). The sisters from the Episcopalian community will be buried in its churchyard – though they did comment that they would be buried on the landward side, as incomers. The seaward side is reserved for native islanders.

The founder of the Episcopalian monastic community, which has been on the island for around twenty-five years, is also a priest, and celebrates the Eucharist in the little church looking out over the sea.[1] It was an extraordinarily focused service, and the hymns we sang emphasised the beauty of creation, which we could observe there and then through the plain glass windows. This coming together of liturgy and natural beauty reminded me of a liturgy celebrated in the Cave of the Apocalypse on Patmos, where tradition has it that St John received the revelation. The church there is small and it was crowded with pilgrims and the local boys who had come to sing, and it became very hot. Then, someone opened a window, and – as on the Scottish island – there was a marvellous experience of praising God in the presence of a window onto extraordinary natural beauty.

Yet ... on Patmos I had been able to receive communion, while in Scotland I could not, not because of the Episcopalians, but because of the rules of my own church. As we have seen with Mary, this eucharistic disunity can be a source of great distress to people, who find themselves unable to receive communion with friends and even family. In my own case, the fact that I was Orthodox meant that I was unable to receive communion at the funerals of my mother and my aunt, at my brother's bedside when he was dying, at his funeral, or even at the Requiem Mass said for my husband by an Anglican priest.

Apart from such personal anomalies, awareness of belonging to something larger is very important, and should be important, for many Christians, and the disunity at a higher level is often disconcerting for people on the ground.

This first became a real issue in my own life in the mid-1990s. I was by then a member of a local Orthodox community that combined a parish under the Ecumenical Patriarchate (Constantinople/Istanbul) with a parish under the Moscow Patriarchate (Russian

Orthodox Church) in one community, sharing a common building. It was a heady mix of people committed to preserving the Orthodox liturgical and spiritual tradition, and people drawn to that and discovering richness there.

Then, in 1996, the Russian Orthodox Church broke communion with the Ecumenical Patriarchate over the Church in Estonia, which had placed itself under Constantinople during the communist era. The rights and wrongs of the dispute are not our concern here. The effect on our community, however, was that people who had experienced themselves as one in Christ (for all our differences and the many arguments that went on in the course of community life) were no longer in communion with each other. All of a sudden, our clergy were not supposed to concelebrate with each other, or give communion to people who – simply for technical reasons as far as most of us were concerned – belonged to the other jurisdiction. Close friends discovered that they were separated from each other by a quarrel that had taken place the other side of the world. Our ecclesial unity with people we had never met was unbroken, and, as far as the church was concerned, was more important than our unity with people we knew intimately, in that it was the former that was able to make it impossible for us to receive communion together.

This situation was resolved quite quickly, but what became apparent to me as a result of the episode was that most of the schism that goes on between churches begins at this kind of level: disagreements not over what we believe, or the nature of the sacraments, but over the nature of authority (to put it nicely) or power (to put it less nicely). The accusations of heresy and so on follow on afterwards – the theology follows the behaviour and not the other way round. This is true even of the East–West division of the eleventh century, which was essentially political. The Orthodox and Catholics do not regard each other's orders or sacraments as 'invalid'. They simply do not celebrate them together or share them. It is perfectly acceptable for an Orthodox to receive communion from a Catholic or vice versa in an emergency, such as on a desert island. The body is broken over issues of authority, and it is these issues that threaten the unity of the Orthodox Churches – and underlie the disunity between East and West – today. This is not to say that these issues are not important – how we understand the structure of the churches has a profound influence on how we understand the nature of church itself – but they belong in the immanent/social corner of our 'map', not to the whole picture.

After the patriarchal rift over Estonia had been healed, my own community returned to the status quo: a highly diverse group of people who disagreed about many things, but who nevertheless experienced themselves as deeply bound together by communion.

An even more perplexing situation arose about ten years later. In 2006, following a major division in the UK diocese of the Russian Orthodox Church, our parish voted by a large majority to leave the Russian Church and place itself within the West European branch of the Ecumenical Patriarchate. This resulted in a hugely painful, and totally unexpected, split in our local Orthodox community, since some of the members of the parish decided to stay with the Russian Church and founded a separate local parish under the Moscow Patriarchate. A period of chaos and confusion led to bitter divisions (of 'the church I go to and the one I wouldn't be seen dead in' variety) and eventually to litigation over property. For everyone involved the conflicts were very real, and shot through with a sense of deep personal betrayal on both sides, going way beyond the everyday conflicts we were used to living with. It was puzzling to realise that while I would be unable to receive communion from dear and trusted friends who were Anglican or Catholic priests, there would be nothing canonically to stop me doing so from people on the other side of a bitter legal dispute. There was no break in communion between the Ecumenical Patriarchate, to which I belonged, and the Russian Orthodox Church. I was 'in communion' with people I was only likely to meet in court, and who cut me dead when I met them in the street, and not in communion with people I loved.

This was very challenging to my understanding – and experience – of the Eucharist. For decades we had experienced communion as transcending ordinary day-to-day personal difficulties. There had been many liturgies where I had gone in feeling quite hostile towards another person, or aware that they felt quite hostile towards me, only to find such feelings had evaporated by the end of the service. Here, however, there existed between the two parts of what had once been one parish such a powerful and unresolved rift in relationship at a human level, not just between individuals but between groups, that it was difficult to comprehend how the liturgy could meaningfully be celebrated together. Alongside the pain was the uncomfortable awareness that we had all prayed together and received communion together for many years: yet it was clear that a huge amount of work would be necessary at a human level before it would be possible for us to come together in the liturgy. Some early attempts at the latter were made, but they only made matters worse. For the time being, at least, although the Eucharist continued to be at the heart of our (separate) church lives, it could no longer unite us. It had ceased to function as a point of convergence at the personal level, even though there was, whether we liked it or not, convergence at the higher, inter-church level.

Though difficult, my inability to receive communion on the Scottish island or at the family funerals was of a different order entirely, because here it was at the inter-church level where the point of convergence failed to function: at the personal level there would have been no problem at all. On each of those occasions I took part in a prayerful, attentive celebration of the Eucharist, celebrated by a priest who had consciously dedicated his or her life to God many years before. A God of love who could find such a Eucharist unacceptable or 'invalid' would be, to me, more incomprehensible than the God who is 'uncircumscribed, without beginning and beyond speech'.

I was, however, willing to observe the boundaries of the wider church on the basis of what I had been told when I was first received into the Orthodox Church. This places the rift in communion back where it belongs – in the immanent social part of our 'map' – and accepts that there are problems that will not go away this side of the parousia. It was explained to me that it is simply a fact that in this world the body of the Church is broken, and is as yet unable to discover its true unity in Christ (the transcendent unity which nothing can in fact break). Until we can manage to make that unity an immanent reality, I was told – and this will not be until the end of time – we should not anticipate it: we *should* be (uncomfortably) aware of our inability to worship together as one.

Is it possible to include everyone?

The Anglican Church – whose orders are not recognised by the Orthodox or the Catholics – have pioneered an open policy where they will welcome anyone to communion who is a communicant member of their own church. This is a bold and positive move, and one that means a great deal to a great many people as a real attempt at overcoming the scandal of disunity. There is a fundamental sense, however, in which it is problematic. A standard form of words is, 'You are invited to receive communion if you are communicant member of your own church. If you are not a communicant member, please come forward to receive a blessing.' In a curious way, this formula undermines, or rather bypasses, the ecclesiological understanding of both the Orthodox and the Catholics, while at the same time accepting their disciplines: for example, a divorced and remarried Catholic would not be able to receive communion in these circumstances.

As an Orthodox, while I recognise that the Anglican approach is a welcoming and much valued invitation, even the suggestion that those who are not receiving communion go up for a blessing presents me personally with a puzzle. It confuses two things – communion and blessing – which are actually quite separate. I am a communicant member of a church where it is quite normal to be at the liturgy and not receive communion, in which case you don't join the queue for communion. This does not mean that you are not participating deeply in the service. In some ways, then, I would feel more excluded by joining the communicants and not receiving communion than I would if I were to stay quietly in my pew and pray.

At a practical level, this practice created difficulties for an Orthodox priest who celebrated a liturgy where there were many Anglicans present. They understood that they would not be given communion, but according to Anglican practice most of them came forward for a blessing. Since an Orthodox priest giving communion is holding a chalice in one hand a spoon with another, he has no free hand with which to bless a person.

This priest was also confused at a deeper level. He was used to celebrating liturgies where people might or might not come to communion, and the not-coming could be as significant as the coming. Not coming to communion could mean that the person felt insufficiently prepared, or was engaged in something that they felt to be incompatible with communion, or had not fasted beforehand, or some other reason, but they were nevertheless fully present to the liturgy. At the end they would receive the *antidoron* (bread that has been blessed but not consecrated) and a blessing from the celebrant. Communion and blessing both took place in the service, but at different times: everyone received the blessing, but only those taking communion received communion, and these were two different things. Anything and anyone can be blessed, and indeed anyone can bless, but only the church community shares communion. In a strange way, then, rather like the 'dual integrity' over women priests, the Anglican approach can be seen as creating a new exclusion, of those who have a different understanding.

For members of churches with a strong sense of ecclesiology, the 'open door' policy can also create difficulties if they like to join in with Anglican worship but sincerely respect that their own church is not in communion with the Anglican Church. A Catholic student had a serious argument with her college chaplain over a communion service in the college chapel. Although she was a chapel warden and attended the morning and evening prayer daily, she had told the chaplain that she 'did not do communion services in chapel': she already went to Mass daily at a local Catholic church, and, in any case would not be able to receive communion at the college Eucharist. It was not, for her, a question of validity, or of the college chaplain being a woman: it was simply that the service was not a Catholic service, and she was painfully aware of a difference in the underlying beliefs. 'I find it very hard', she said, 'being at a Church of England communion service, using the same words, believing in transubstantiation, and I am not one of them and they know that I am not. It gets to me and distracts me, and I end up fretting about that rather than praying. I feel the pain of not being in communion.' The fact that the chaplain had said 'she didn't care if I stood on my head in a corner as long as I turned up' led to a painful disagreement which, fortunately, was soon resolved. What was needed was for the chaplain to understand that in order to be truly inclusive she needed to take into account how genuinely painful the disunity of the churches was for this particular student.

Unity in diversity?

Whatever the subtleties of people's liturgical understanding, it is nevertheless clear that the disunity of the churches causes enormous scandal and distress. 'Lack of unity is the single biggest problem,' said a lay pastoral worker in an Anglican church. She had been told many times by fundamentalists that she was not a Christian because she had liberal attitudes, something she found 'increasingly irritating'.

The ecumenical movement has, of course, taken great strides in some areas in recent decades, and one aspect of this is what is called 'positive ecumenism'. Instead of each defining ourselves as the one true church, waiting for the others to see the error of their ways, we accept that each tradition has its particular riches, and we look to see what each can offer the other. Seen in this way, it could be said that the fragmentation of the churches is a good thing. It means each person can find what is best for them, the way to worship which seems to them most meaningful. We do need in some sense to feel at home in our church community. It needs to be secure and familiar enough to allow us to let go of our day-to-day preoccupations.

As human beings we have a profound need to know where and who we are, and since we are so diverse this feeds our human tendency to split into factions. A young friend who works at Smithfield Market in London says that there are bitter divisions between the vegetarians, the vegans and the raw food people. Sharing dislike of another group is tremendously bonding, and this binds together church communities as well as secular ones.

One might hope that the Christian churches would be able to go beyond this. We may always be searching for security and clear boundaries, but Christ constantly knocks them down. In the Parable of the Talents (Matthew 25:14ff.), he tells us that reward is not dependent on how much work we have done; he constantly breaks through the laws of ritual purity that were so strong in the religious society of his day; ultimately he even breaks the barrier of death.

At a human level, however, we are caught up in our own fragmentation. Only Christ can embrace all in all, and for us every inclusion creates a new exclusion. When we make a conscious effort to include a particular person or group, this is important, but it also carries the risk that we immediately create new borders that exclude others. The emergence of a previously unheard voice can mean, as at Pentecost, a genuine movement towards everyone hearing in their own language – or it can simply mean the silencing of others.

For example, in an article entitled 'The Bumbling Pastoral Worker', Jenny Gaffin describes working with a group that was multifaith, lesbian, gay, bisexual and transsexual – surely a remarkably inclusive group by most people's standards. Hearing the pain of exclusion that had been experienced in many situations by the members of this group, she became determined 'to create a theology of inclusivity so watertight that nobody would have any justification for prejudice of any kind'. She quickly found that this was simply impossible: ' "Inclusive" simply means including the people who share our values, rather than including everybody.'

> The closest we came to identifying a set of goals or ground rules came through an assumption summarised by Revd Bernard Lynch, a Catholic Priest: 'obviously there would have to be, and is within our group, a total agreement that anything that would be injurious, physically, psychologically, spiritually, of the self or other could not be part of our struggle for freedom'. Underlying this ideal was the realisation that we ourselves were guilty of exclusion. In some cases this exclusion was quite conscious: one participant in the groups asked, in reference to the right wing strands of her religious tradition, 'Why do I have to talk to a bunch of fundamentalist nutcases?' At other times, the exclusion was more subtle, based on unspoken assumptions about gender or sexual norms.[2]

The point Gaffin makes clear here is that, try as we might, we cannot as human beings get beyond our separateness – we can only try to become constantly more aware of our assumptions and constantly more respectful and understanding of other people. Sometimes this may involve simply accepting and respecting our separateness, as argued by Jonathan Sacks in his recent book, *The Home We Build Together*. Sacks's central question in the book is: how do we move on from multi-culturalism without moving back to a single dominant culture in which it is all too easy to be 'not one of us'. The solution, he suggests, is a covenantal model where we look together at our needs and resources and agree how they can best be used for the good of everyone:

> Covenant entered the West through religion, but is not an essentially religious concept. An analogy is forgiveness, which also began life as a religious idea, which now addresses all of us, regardless of faith. Thinking in terms of covenant does not presuppose an actual, historical agreement any more than social contract presupposes an actual, historical contract. It is simply a way of thinking, a habit of heart and mind that shapes our understanding of social realities.[3]

These needs extend also, of course, into situations where people of different faiths worship together. Michael was involved in arranging an anniversary service for the hospital where he works, at a local Anglican cathedral. Since the patients were of various faith backgrounds the organisers invited an imam and a rabbi to give blessings at the end of the service. He was deeply embarrassed by the insistence of the cathedral staff in separating out the blessings given by them from that given by the Christian priest. 'The cathedral staff didn't refuse to let them do the blessing but they refused to allow them to give their blessings in the same frame as the Christian one. There had to be a hymn after the Christian blessings before the imam and the rabbi did theirs. I just wanted to put a bomb under it – it is such a trivialisation. If we can't break apart this idea that Christianity is the one true thing, it just feels completely hopeless. If the global situation is operating on the level of [...] Cathedral, we are completely done for.'

What Michael is arguing for here is not a relativisation of what we believe, but a faith that does not need to be defensive, that fully respects the beliefs of others, and accepts our own shortcomings. As the church, as the embodiment of Christ's' personal presence, we are at the cutting edge of all the dimensions of our lives that converge in the Eucharist: we stand between the spiritual and the material, between the personal and the social. While in one sense the mystery of the incarnation has already taken place, in another it is as yet incomplete, and we are part of the incompleteness. We are, as church, the fullness of Christ himself who 'fills all in all' (Ephesians 1:23), but as such we are entirely inadequate to the task.

Accepting this kind of limitation was, perhaps, the particular contribution of the myrrh-bearing women who came to Christ's tomb on Easter morning. It was they who expressed the continuity of love, even in the face of death. When they came to the tomb that morning the group of disciples were scattered. The body of the church was perhaps at that moment as broken as it has ever been. Yet it was still possible to do the ordinary loving thing that women normally did for a person who had died, and it was in doing that, in going to pay 'the gentlest attention' to the body of Jesus, that the resurrection was revealed.[4]

For some people the differences they find in the churches and the wounds that are inflicted are too great. For others the benefits they receive outweigh the difficulties. Our next concern is with those who stay knowing how bad it can be, who are themselves wounded and betrayed, as Christ was wounded and betrayed, but somehow remain within the body that itself requires so much gentleness and love to be healed. First, however, we need to think a little about how these wounds come about.

What does it mean to be church?

9

The problem of the 'feel-good factor'

That the Body of Christ – the church – is wounded and fragmented should hardly surprise us. The resurrection of Jesus was not a return to the situation before his death, and it did not show that everything was suddenly all right again. His resurrected body carried the wounds of the violence that had been perpetrated at his death. When he ascended, taking our human nature with him into heaven, he still carried those wounds in his body. In this world, the church will never be about everything being 'OK': it has to live in a world populated by us, who have such a powerful propensity to identify over against other people in order to make ourselves feel secure. We easily turn to violence. Being in that world, and being made up of us, the church is in constant danger of falling into the same trap. 'The church', said one woman, 'allows a lot of reactionary people with views that are full of hate to have a place where they can feel themselves justified and better than other people. People inside the church are actually nastier than people outside.' This is a common perception, and one that we need to take seriously.

Does the coming of Jesus bring great joy, healing and wonder into the world? Yes, of course it does. But in the wake of that joy and wonder come rivalry, betrayal and death. Why? Not because that is what God wants, but because that is the structure of our condition: it is the way we operate.

As we have seen in Chapter 3, people are drawn into the church not only by inner promptings, but by seeing that something matters to other people. Yes, there is the inner search, but we are also attracted by seeing others living a particular kind of life, or being in possession of something that we do not understand but that is clearly desirable to them. In our own times, when church services are open to everyone, it is hard to imagine the extraordinary power of the barrier that once existed between the not-yet-baptised catechumenate and those who had been initiated into the mysteries of the church, into the Eucharist. Being excluded from something can, of course, be a very strong stimulus to desire. It is rare nowadays to see the non-baptised dismissed from the Eucharist at the end of the liturgy of the word, before the 'mysteries' take place, but an Anglican priest told me this was still the practice when he was a naval rating in the 1950s. Being dismissed before the eucharistic part of the service instilled in him a sense that what the others had must be really worth having, and this, he felt, had been influential in his eventually becoming a priest. When Celia and Jill were impressed by the gentleness of the nuns at their convent schools, when Jeffrey was attracted by the group of Christians he met at university, when Claire realised her friend who had remained in the church was 'a decent human' being, they not only perceived something desirable in these people, but wanted what those people had: they experienced the call of Christ through them, and they also wanted to be more like them.

Imitation and discipleship

So far, so good. We are born imitators (how else would we ever learn how to interact with other people?), and we have a propensity to learn what is desirable through seeing what other people think is desirable (how else would the advertising industry survive?). What happens, though, when we all want the same thing? This is a core problem in discipleship. Let us take two talented musicians, Susan and Philip. Susan is middle-aged and has for many years led the choir of a particular parish. A lifelong church member, her approach to church music is not only musical but infused with a life of prayer. She loves the work, and communicates her enthusiasm easily to others. Philip is in his early thirties, an adult convert, and is deeply impressed by Susan. He likes and admires her and wants to become more like her. Susan's infectious enthusiasm for church music, and her evident enjoyment in being a choirmaster, shows Philip that such a position is highly desirable. What marks Philip out from the other people in the choir is that he, too, is musically talented. He has some of the same spiritual qualities that Susan has which make it possible to pray through music. Above all, being in some ways like her, he is a position to recognise her qualities in a particular way.

Susan recognises his qualities in return and Philip is delighted when she brings him into her intimate circle, and gives him every opportunity to learn from her. He rapidly absorbs the particular musical tradition of that parish, and develops skills as a choirmaster. Susan is less alone, and has the gratification of an able and willing pupil; Philip has the gratification of being seen by the choir and congregation to be in the same mould as his model, Susan. Each encourages the other, just as Jill described in her journey with the church. At this stage, however, as Susan's disciple Philip is imitating her at a relatively superficial level. He has learned her trade, but he is a man, she is a woman; they are very different in terms of age and life experience, and what he brings to being a choirmaster is quite different from what she brings. If he sticks too closely, then, to what she has taught him, without bringing his own self to it, he is in danger of becoming, as choirmaster, simply a clone of Susan.

At this stage, Philip's situation is perhaps comparable to that of the seventy sent out by Jesus in Luke 10 who discover that they can heal people and drive out demons in his name. They are understandably excited: 'Lord, even the demons are subject to us in your name!' – we can do it too! And he reminds them not to 'rejoice that the spirits are subject to you; but rejoice that your names are written in heaven' (Luke 10:20). They have to be reminded that what is marvellous is not that they have acquired some kind of magic power, by which they can imitate Jesus' acts of healing, but the fact that the spirits respond to them in this way means they are truly in touch with what Jesus has revealed to them. Jesus goes on to thank the Father for this.

Philip's problem, of course, is a little different. While there are endless demons needing to be cast out, there are only so many church choirs, and only one in his parish. If he can do what Susan does, it is difficult for him not to begin to wonder why he should not have her job, or part of it. It is at this stage that his admiration is in danger of turning to envy. He also presents a problem for Susan, who is well aware that she now has a rival. Yet they are fond of each other, and they are both people of prayer operating within a non-rivalrous Christian framework. If Philip is to continue to be Susan's disciple, like the seventy, he has to understand that his imitation of her must take place at a deeper level than it has so far. What she reveals to him is not just an enviable life as a choirmaster, but a particular relationship to her musical gifts which involves bringing her whole personality and life experience to what is essentially a prayerful offering. Once he begins to imitate her at this level, the rivalry is immediately reduced, since, while drawing on what he has learned from her, he becomes, as a very different person, a very different kind of choirmaster. Much of what he does may still be recognisably in the tradition Susan has taught him, but he is no longer a clone. The tradition is living through him.

This, in turn, presents Susan with a problem. What is her relationship to the tradition she has taught him? Does she simply want him to be able to direct a choir 'in her name' as it were, or is she prepared to risk allowing it to develop, as it inevitably will, in Philip's hands? At the same time, the stable situation which has existed for years, that Susan runs the choir, and there is no one anywhere near as good as her at it, is disturbed. Philip-as-clone did not seriously threaten the equilibrium, but Philip-as-living-tradition does. Susan's is not the only way of doing it, and she is no longer the only authority. And if Philip can learn to do it, and do it a bit differently, some choir members may be thinking, 'Maybe some of us could, too'. The choir itself becomes a less comfortable place to be, and there is a good chance of a split developing between those who would like to restore the status quo by getting rid of Philip, and those who feel Susan has had her day and ought to retire gracefully. Anyone familiar with church life will, at this point, be able to see trouble ahead, but we don't need to go there. This scenario is simply to illustrate how easily envy can set in when we set out to imitate someone we genuinely like and admire, and this was precisely Jesus' problem: 'it was out of envy that they delivered him' – even Pilate could see this (Matthew 27:18).

Jesus also brought with him a further problem. Although many people were healed and began to understand the love of God through him, far from righting all the wrongs, his presence was subversive: he overturned a great many presuppositions. He not only drew people to him, but he inspired envy, anxiety, discomfort, and he constantly criticised the religious authorities of the time in ways that often resonate powerfully with the complaints made about the church today. This would have been bad enough if he were just another prophet, but he also claimed to put an end to prophecy, to be the Son of God. What his persecutors could not see, and what Judas could not see, was that he was not just another religious teacher in competition with the others: he was beyond rivalry. Being fully God as well as fully human he knew there was enough to go around. He had no need to cling on to power, or to rival or envy his disciples as they began to take on board what he was telling them. He could simply rejoice in the deepening revelation. As they grew, so did the presence of God in the world. This is what Judas so disastrously misunderstood, when salvation did not seem to be happening in a way that he could identify. For him, as for the authorities, Jesus became a problem.

In a story by the Catholic writer Flannery O'Connor, there is a violent criminal known as 'The Misfit'. Caught out in an act of murder he complains that by raising the dead, 'Jesus thrown everything off balance.'[1] Jesus may do good, but he upsets our normal understanding of how things are. It makes us feel unsafe, so we fall back on trying to restore a world where we know where we are: a world with 'the rich man in his castle and the poor man at his gate', about whom we used to sing in the 1950s: 'God made them high and lowly and ordered their estate.'[2] The Gospel Jesus preached was radical. It was a Gospel of generosity, where God so much wants to give to us that there is no satisfying – or safe – relationship between virtue and reward. The Prodigal is welcomed with open arms simply because he has come back. The older brother is no less loved because of this – but he is no more loved either, because God's love is not conditional on anything but our capacity to receive it. The Pharisee who prayed a prayer of gratitude that he 'was not as other men are' (Luke 18:9ff.) was not a bad man. He did all the right things. But he was less receptive to God's love than the tax collector who understood only too well that he was in need of God's mercy.

When our ordinary understanding of the way the world is is disturbed – when we realise that Susan is not the only person who can direct the choir, or that Philip represents a threat to the way things have always been – we naturally seek to restore order. For human beings, there is hardly anything so bonding as a common enemy. When our equilibrium is disturbed, the desire to join in with the others who have identified what 'the problem' is, and therefore appear to hold the key to setting things right, easily takes over. The most valuable history lesson I ever had at school was given by an English woman who had been in Germany as a student in the late 1930s. She understood this process completely, and made a brave statement to a class of enlightened 1960s girls about an experience when she got caught up in the crowd: 'Never be too confident in your ability to stand up for what is right,' she told us. 'When I stood there in the crowds, shouting "Heil Hitler", it was completely intoxicating. It would not have mattered what I thought or believed.' She was not talking about a simple failure of courage. What she was trying to get across to us is that in the intoxication of a crowd mentality you come to believe what the crowd believes, to want what the crowd wants, just as the crowd who shouted for the crucifixion of Jesus had come to want that more than anything else. Caught up in communal condemnation of almost anything we feel restored to ourselves, and this is very often what we do as church. We read a 'feel-good factor' into the gospels: *we* are going to be all right, and everyone else, the nuisance people, will be cast out. A church that was meant to be for everyone becomes 'my church'.

The devastating effect of the 'feel-good' factor

Likewise, if we are not careful, we get drawn into the idea that what the crucifixion represents is a setting aright of this kind. God became angry, Jesus came and endured the punishment for our sins, God was appeased, and is on our side again – so long as we know what's what and behave ourselves. So much Christian teaching is based on this fundamental misunderstanding. It was Christians, for example, who triggered the 'Atheist Bus Campaign'. The campaign began in June 2008 when the *Guardian* website published a blog about Christian adverts running on London buses. Ariane Sherine, the originator of the blog, visited a website address included in the advertisement. On this website, she wrote:

> *I received the following warning for anyone who doesn't 'accept the word of Jesus on the cross': 'You will be condemned to everlasting separation from God and then you spend all eternity in torment in hell. Jesus spoke about this as a lake of fire which was prepared for the devil and all his angels (demonic spirits)' (Matthew 25:41). Lots to look forward to, then.*[3]

Sherine's response was to propose that atheists reading her article could each donate £5 to fund a reassuring counter-advert. The idea quickly caught on, and within three months £135,000 had been raised. By January 2009, around eight hundred buses were carrying adverts with the slogan 'There's probably no God. Now stop worrying about it, and enjoy your life.'

The atheist slogan is remarkably similar to what the Misfit goes on to say in O'Connor's story: 'If He [Jesus] did what He said, then it's nothing for you to do but to throw away everything and follow Him, and if He didn't, then it's nothing for you to do but enjoy the few minutes you got left the best way you can.'[4] What both The Misfit and the bus poster miss is the obvious: that God is not life-destroying but life-creating. God is not setting out to make life unpleasant for us, but recognises that life is unpleasant in a fallen world, and enters into it, sharing all the consequences. This is important because it is here that a major misunderstanding creeps in, of the 'God wanted Jesus dead' variety. God did not want Jesus dead: he wanted all of us alive, and since human beings were (and are) incapable of overcoming death, the only way to deal with this was to become one of us and to go through the whole process, not calling on the protection of angels or divine power to wipe out the enemy, but going through the middle of it.

Jesus reveals the love of God to us, but he also reveals to us who we are, and he does this in two ways. First, he is a model for what we could (should?) be like: the 'second Adam' (1 Corinthians 15:22). Whereas Adam was created in Paradise, however, Christ is born into a fallen world. He is tempted by, and subject to, all the temptations of a fallen world, but his human will, though a free will, is totally aligned to his divine will, which is one with the will of the Father. When, in Gethsemane, Jesus says 'Thy will not mine be done', this is not about God wanting some kind of punitive satisfaction, but about following through that other aspect of revealing to us what we are like. On the one hand, Jesus is someone for us to imitate: he is a human being as originally created. On the other hand, by going through Gethsemane, through trial and death, he reveals to us our own violence. But a message of ultimate love – of God being not just on our side but on everyone's side – is too costly in terms of society's structures. We are constantly tempted to defend ourselves against it.

The crucifixion: 'a judgement of judgement'

Far from some kind of argument between Jesus and God the Father as between a child and an authority figure, it is this healing that is going on in Gethsemane. There *is* a conflict of wills, but it is between the free human will of Jesus, which would like to back out of the whole thing, for obvious reasons, and the divine will of Jesus that is totally aligned with the outpouring love of God, and desires to follow through the consequences of living in a fallen world in order to redeem that world. In accepting the cross, he brings his human will into alignment with his divine will in an act of complete trust that God's love can transcend the hideous consequences of violence.

The crucifixion is not then a judgement of Jesus, as representing the human race. It is, as the sixth-century monk Maximos the Confessor said, 'a judgement of judgement':[5] it reveals what happens when we cling on to our need for security, seeking out scapegoats. Sadly, this revelation is easily distorted, so as to breed guilt, self-hatred, and – consequently – more violence.

Kate was brought up in a church family where she was severely punished for any bad behaviour, for example by being locked in a dark cupboard for hours on end. She and her brother were also physically punished by their father. God became for her the terrifying and punitive father and Christ the one who suffered for her sins. This did not make her feel loved by Christ: in fact it made her feel condemned, and the burden of guilt that went with this was so painful that once she left home she kept well away from anything religious. Like Claire, in Chapter 2, she felt cast out. Through a series of relationships she gradually began to feel better about herself, and the violence that had been turned against herself began, instead, to be turned against Christ. Whenever she saw an image of Christ on the cross she experienced feelings of violent hatred: 'It was as though he was up there saying, "How evil you are, and how good I am: see how I suffer for you." It seemed so – well – manipulative. It made me want to get in there and hammer in the nails myself.'

Eventually Kate married and had a child, and the guilt that had dogged her since childhood began to heal. As this happened, Kate slowly began to experience the crucifixion differently: 'It began, I suppose, when I had a child of my own. Her perceptions were so fresh. We did not go to church, but we lived near a church where there was a large crucifix outside. One day we were walking past and my daughter said to me (she was about five at the time), "What's that?" I said it was Jesus on the cross, and she said, "Why would anyone want to do that to someone?" It brought me up short. It was the first time I realised just how horrible a thing it was to do to anyone.'

Some years later, while visiting her parents, Kate felt a stirring of curiosity about what Christians actually believed. She idly flipped through a Bible that was in the house, and started reading the Beatitudes:[6] 'There was a crucifix on the wall of my parent's sitting room, and as I read, this image began to seem terrible in a different way from before. The Beatitudes are so encouraging, so loving. And it seemed dreadful that the person who said those things should end up as he did. It went on from there. I had these images of this little baby born into the world, and of Jesus, this healer and prophet – and then the crucifixion. I realised for the first time what a terrifying thing the crucifixion is because it shows what love does to us. We can't bear it and we try to destroy it. Love is so much more difficult to deal with than hatred.' What Kate describes here is a growing understanding of the gospel story that moves from a 'law court' model of *atonement* – that we were so wicked someone had to die to appease God – to an understanding of *at-one-ment*. In the incarnation God entered the created world, in history, as an act of solidarity: to bring about a healing of the division between himself and creation, including human beings.

This in no way belittled the problems. Rather it revealed them. When Jesus was being tormented and crucified, he did not pretend that nothing bad was going on, and a refusal to identify over against others does not mean we do away with a distinction between right and wrong. 'Father, forgive,' says Jesus when he is being nailed to the cross, 'for they know not what they do.' Not, 'They can't help it because of their background'; not, 'They are only doing what they think is right'; not, 'If I can endure this everything will be all right'; not even, 'Being a superior person I can rise above this.' The point is that he knew more about what these people were doing than they knew themselves. They were caught up in routine, everyday violence. He knew that something unspeakably terrible was being done: human beings were murdering their own Creator and God. When he asked God the Father to forgive them because of their ignorance, it made the deed no less terrible in itself. Within that request lies hidden the unthinkable consequences should these people not somehow be forgiven. Their crime was so appalling that forgiveness was the only possible outcome that would not end in utter destruction. At the same time, he did not say '*I* forgive you'. He handed the situation to the Father.

A man who had spent years recovering a sense of wholeness after a breakdown that resulted from emerging memories of being sexually abused as a child demonstrated how this can happen in ordinary life. Asked how he felt about the man who did this to him, he said, 'First of all I had to let him reduce to his own size. He had been so huge in my consciousness. Then, I had to restore him to the community – the communion of saints. Whatever he did was not ultimately to do with me, but between him and God.'

This man had achieved a remarkable degree of freedom from the damage that had been done to him. It could be said that he had reached a level of at-one-ment within himself whereby, like Christ on the cross, he was able to hand the situation to God. The wounds he had received were no longer driving the way he lived. They were real; they still made him especially vulnerable in certain situations; but in the theatre of his mind, they had ceased to be the only show in town. He was, at least in part, free.

From this point, perhaps, we can begin to look at what it might mean to try to undo the defences we discussed in Chapter 6; to acknowledge the woundedness and fragmentation of the church while still maintaining faith in the core message.

10

Living within the wounds of Christ's body

It is clear that in our first two senses of 'Church on Trial' – trying it on for size, and seeing how it is behaving – there can be no verdict. We have seen that it is a power for good in people's lives, and that it is valued for its very existence in society. We have also seen that a lot of the time it falls short of preaching or living out its own message, and that people get badly hurt. All this is predictable. It is also clear that Christianity is not a solitary path: each person's journey is unique but it is lived out in relation to other people. Even a monastic (Christian) hermit, though they may be physically and socially on the edge of the church, is deeply involved not just in a personal relationship with God but with the prayer of the body – of the church itself. Furthermore, according to the model presented in this book we do not have a choice about whether there should be church or not: for Christians it is built into God's presence in the world. We do, of course, have choices about how we relate to its various manifestations.

Some people find the kinds of things that happen to people in church life – and the relations between the churches – deeply shocking; others shrug and say, 'That is how it is.' My experience is that the further the listener is from any kind of church membership the more shocked he or she is. For those on the inside, the stories are all too familiar. It is by being on the inside that we become vulnerable to damage, and the greater our involvement the greater our vulnerability. If, as we have suggested, the body of the church requires our gentlest attention, then we, as its members, require that too.

So much of the self-image of the churches involves seeing themselves as holding out their arms to the poor, the damaged, the disenfranchised, providing help and succour to various 'others' – and of course many churches do this, and do it very well. Yet we are all at different times in need of help, and pastoral care, it seems, is too often seen as something done by the churches only for those outside, or as something done by the 'healthy' members of the community for the others, rather than the kind of mutual self-giving we saw in Jill's story.

Not enough attention is paid to the wounds that are inflicted within the very body itself, by individual to individual, by one church to another, or by the organisation to groups and individuals within it. There are those who are falsely accused and never receive justice, who are subject to envy because they manage to serve the church successfully in some way, who are victims of gossip and slander, whose good will is ruthlessly exploited, or whose fragile confidences are easily broken.

At a simple level, it is common for a parishioner to confide in a priest about something that fills him or her with shame, only to find that very problem the subject of next Sunday's sermon. Similarly, a young man spoke to his vicar about the stirrings of a fragile vocation to the priesthood. The very next Sunday, the vicar, unable to contain his pride, announced to the congregation that the young man was seeking ordination.

Every parish will know people who have become too old, too forgetful, too ill or too stressed to carry out duties they have faithfully fulfilled for years – as churchwardens, organists, tea-makers, cleaners and so on. The community will watch them failing, and no one will dare address the subject with the person concerned. Suddenly a substitute is discovered, and the person finds him- or herself usurped and discarded overnight. It is not, of course, that people should be allowed to abuse the system by hanging on to roles they can no longer fulfil: the complaint here is that there tends to be a great lack of courage in helping a person in this situation face up to what is going on, and the result is too often not only that they are dropped without warning, but also they never receive due thanks for all they have done. The failure lies in there being no will to confront these situations truthfully. 'I am the only one who dares to address issues,' said one woman, 'and you end up such a target. You look a fool – and you look as if you are causing the problems when you are addressing them.'

Again, great value is given to endurance, to self-giving: so great that it is rare for anyone to be offered help when a particular duty is becoming too much, perhaps because of illness, or life changes such as bereavement. There are few who know how to ask for support, and even fewer who dare suggest it for fear of losing a responsibility which means a great deal to them. So they struggle on, until the situation collapses, and has to be picked up by someone else. 'Time and again in church situations,' said a woman who had spent years as a churchwarden, 'I have tried to avoid this, by training helpers, by sharing the work, by planning, by looking ahead to see where the problems might lie, and time and again I have been defeated. It is almost as though there is a commitment to crisis.'

It is also clear that for all the emphasis on marriage and family life, the churches are often only too ready to ignore the needs of spouses and families of those who work for them, as we have seen in Chapter 5. Very often, of course, we find that clergy themselves are horribly betrayed: when things go wrong, it is so often the people for whom they have most given themselves who most bitterly attack them.

We can be betrayed in our personal relationships with other church members, by the attitude of a community, by particular people in authority – but also by the things that go on within the body itself. Twenty years ago, Tom was a lively young deacon and a gifted jazz musician who enjoyed jam sessions on a Saturday night. He left to work for the church in the USA, and was ordained priest there; recently I met up with him after a long gap. Of course he was older, but he was clearly not very well, and he told me he is on eight different kind of antidepressant. For the last nine years his only leave has been sick leave, and he had recently asked for a year's sabbatical to try to recover his health. He was granted three months. His job? Sifting the accusations of sexual abuse made against his fellow clergy.

In all these situations, the wound inflicted is twofold. There is the damage done to a particular person or people, and there is the damage inflicted on the Body itself – on its unity in the Spirit – by the thoughtlessness or cruelty from within. This itself is bad enough, but there is yet a further wound which affects the Body: the frequent determination to ignore the pain, to apply sticking plaster without salve, so that the wound festers and grows beneath it. Situations which would never be tolerated in secular organisations are covered up in the name of forgiveness: cheap grace, cheap reconciliation. Avril spoke of a time when she had been badly hurt by a man in her congregation who lied about her to other people and spread rumours that she was having an affair with someone she had never even thought about in those terms. It had badly damaged her reputation in the church community, and caused a number of people to treat her as beyond the pale. In a church group she came under pressure to 'forgive and forget'; she tried to explain that she was hurt by this man's behaviour, and would appreciate it if he could at least apologise and set the record straight publicly, which there had been no attempt to do. 'I am angry with him,' she confessed. 'But do you love him?', asked one of the group. 'What kind of question was that?', asked Avril when she told this story, 'It had nothing to do with whether I loved him or not. I simply wanted the hurt acknowledged so that I could move on.'

When we are hurt, certain biblical phrases tend to ring in our ears, even if they are not thrown at us by our fellow Christians: 'Turn the other cheek', 'Love your enemies', 'Forgive unto seventy times seven'. To make use of these, we need to find ways of interpreting them which do not turn into simple denial.

One of the greatest revelations ever made to me by a priest was his statement, 'When you are hurt, you shout.' This is so obvious, but is it what we see happening? It is considered a classic characteristic of the English that when someone bumps into us, we say 'Sorry'. It is a classic characteristic of many Christians, too. When hurt, we feel unable to shout, we go quiet, we ponder on what has happened and try to convince ourselves we have forgiven what has been done, when we have not even begun to face it.

One of the key insights of psychoanalysis is the idea that we are so frightened of our own anger that when someone hurts us we go to great lengths to protect them from it. This has nothing to do with forgiveness. When it happens, we are simply afraid, and it is easier to turn the anger inwards against oneself than to place it where it belongs. One of the most valuable understandings of melancholia or depression provided by Freud is that a state of depression means that we are angry with a person we love, or feel we should love, and cannot allow ourselves to be so. All our energy, then, is taken up with suppressing that anger, and we have none left for everyday life. It may be that our anger is unreasonable, for example when someone we love has died and the anger stems from a sense of being abandoned; or it may be that it is a natural reaction to a betrayal or hurt inflicted by another. In either case, the anger is real, and unless it is allowed expression it will compound the damage within.

Kevin, a Roman Catholic, was devastated by the death of his younger brother, and felt very angry with some people who had been indirectly involved in it. They had not done anything with intent to kill his brother, but they had acted carelessly, and the brother who died had himself acted recklessly. Kevin could not see his brother as anything but a helpless victim, and the people involved as anything but his murderers. He became obsessed with fantasies of revenge, which he confided in me to the point where I began to become anxious as to whether I would be an accessory, through foreknowledge, to a very serious crime. I broached this with him, and he told me that talking about what he wanted to do was his safety net. As long as I allowed him to talk about what he would like to do to these people, he would not do it. I decided to trust him. Meanwhile, he vented a lot of anger in vigorous sports. As his anger receded, he came to realise that his dead brother was not the saint that the rest of the family now made him out to be. This made no difference to how much he loved and mourned him, but he could see that what had happened was not pure victimisation. It was a combination of ordinary carelessness on the part of the people he had hated, reckless stupidity on the part of his brother, and sheer bad luck. The death had not been an inevitable consequence, by any means, of what had taken place. He trained as a youth worker, and is now a pastoral worker with young people.

Kevin's story demonstrates two aspects of the transformation of injury into a redemptive act. He did not forget or excuse what had been done. He did not deny that a wrong had been committed. Above all he did not rein in his anger, but confronted it, expressed it, fantasised about it. He did, however, stop short of acting on it in a destructive way. We could say he took responsibility for it, and was able to use it instead of letting it take possession of his personality. He was able to turn it against the evil which was at the root of his brother's death, rather than on the people who had got mixed up in it.

It is sometimes said that there are three major barriers to spiritual health – the first is procrastination – assuming there will be plenty of time to start worrying about spiritual matters later on, when we are older; the second is distraction – 'I have married a wife, bought a piece of land, etc.' – and the third is the behaviour of religious authorities and institutions. It is not just that they fail to provide the nourishment we need. When churches and clergy behave badly, or appear to have no regard for the Gospel, or demonstrate a profound lack of compassion or concern for justice, they become a powerful temptation, which goes something like: if that is how the church behaves then there is absolutely no point in trying to belong to it.

Faced with this vision of freedom and relief the voice of conscience whispers, 'But what about ... X who held true to the church throughout years of persecution, Y, a priest of total integrity, Z who has done so much to relieve the burden on people's souls?' Wherever these things go on, there is the church. In Chapter 6, we looked at ways in which we sometimes respond when the event is mightier than the structure: reaching the end of the road; compartmentalising church from the rest of our lives – hiding from ourselves; or excluding ourselves – hiding from the church. Here we will explore some ways in which, with that in mind, people do keep going.

'The baby and the bath water'

Joanna has many reasons to dislike the church. She is a talented artist who was brought up in a very strict church household where art was considered to be not the kind of thing Christians should be involved in. This led her into such conflict that as a young woman she had a breakdown and spent some time in hospital. She recovered and some years later met a man with whom she found a strong and mutual love, but he abandoned her in order to become a celibate priest. Now in her early sixties, she still lives alone; she continues to paint and be involved in a number of local arts projects. In recent years, her parents being long dead, she has returned to the church. Why? 'Out of respect', she said, 'for what I knew was there. I felt I knew myself well enough – was enough myself now – to see what was there and not to be swamped by it. I didn't want to throw the baby out with the bath water.'

What is interesting about Joanna's approach is that, in order to accommodate the church, she has not returned to some former state. Nor has she abandoned everything she grew up with. She has somehow sifted her experience sufficiently to find what is true – and she continues to do so. At first she tried various churches, including a Roman Catholic one where she played the organ for the Sunday Mass, 'which', she added wryly, 'was quite gracious of me since they wouldn't give me communion'. She left there when she moved house, and went to a number of different churches: in one she felt exploited because although again she played the organ and this time she was able to receive to communion, no one ever spoke to her. 'They were a congregation', she said, 'who had been through thick and thin [over the ordination of women], and they simply did not have room for anyone new.' She is now well settled in an Anglican congregation, where she sings in the choir and is very involved in the community life, which has its ups and its downs. As for the worship, 'Of course,' she said, 'much of what you have to say in church could be offensive [referring to one's own guilt and sinfulness] – but I can say to myself, "I know what *I* mean by that: my mother would have heard it differently." ' Joanna, then, has been on an extraordinary journey of integration. She is sure of who she is, she is aware that the church has shortcomings, but she does not let that get in the way of finding there 'the one thing needful'.

Going on being: bringing one's whole self into church

One thing that comes across very clearly in the gospels is that Jesus took people as they were. Sometimes this meant that they did not follow him, as with the 'rich young man' (Mark 10:17–27). What we do not see Jesus doing is trying to change people to fit his requirements – he presents them with the reality of the situation and lets them react. It is a marvellous thing when the church is able to do this, but how often are people put off by expectations around dress, by moralising sermons, even by the prayers themselves.

In Chapter 4 we saw how an argument over dress in church was brought to an end by someone who said, 'The only important thing is that you come to church as yourself.' Whereas I had run into trouble over wearing trousers, a friend of mine – in an Anglican church this time – had problems with her shoes. Nobody complained, as it happens, but she herself was shocked to realise 'I was the only person in church who had high-heeled shoes on. Everyone else walked silently and there was this terrible clip-clop from me. And I thought, "I don't belong here: acoustically I don't belong here."'

How do we deal with a sense that we don't belong? In Chapter 6 we saw how Michael stopped going to church when he was told to lie about his sexuality when he applied for ordination. He simply could not go on with a situation where he was expected to lie about who he was, and wisely concluded that it was not his battle. We could say that this was not a decision to leave the church. What he came up against was a church that, in its dishonesty, was not being church in this situation. As we have seen, by keeping away he in no way lost his faith in the Christian story, and he continued to value the role of the church in bringing people together for worship. Sometimes, for some people, it may be that keeping away from church while maintaining one's faith is an important way of going on being a Christian. Unlike Judas, he did not despair and kill himself. He went on to live as fully himself, believing in God's love for him, even if this meant being pretty well outside the church.

There are others, however, who feel called to be part of change from within. They go beyond compartmentalising those parts of themselves that the church finds unacceptable and insist on bringing them with them. It can be an extremely risky and painful thing to do, but when we do it, attitudes can change and barriers can fall. Alexandra acts as a non-stipendiary minister in a very High Church Anglican parish, where, only fifteen years ago, a young female ordinand on a placement heard herself described as 'a bitch' by some male members of the PCC who did not want a woman priest anywhere near their church. Now, Alexandra is one of several priests – the rest of them male – who take services at this church. She appreciates it for having 'all the important things: good preaching, good music, good liturgy'. All the same, she has not had an easy time: 'There is quite a lot of spite,' she remarked. 'It is very hard to be an Anglo-Catholic woman priest. It's very hard to get training, and very hard to get experience because the Anglo-Catholic churches don't want female curates, so it's a vicious circle.' Of course, she pointed out, once women were being ordained it was always *possible* for her to be ordained too, and she did not have to fight for that. The problems were more subtle: about not being able to apply for certain jobs, about being excluded from certain circles, but she saw this as part of her call to follow Christ: 'A lot of people are marginalised,' she said. 'It goes with being a Christian.'

Asked how she managed to maintain her role, she said, 'I depend very much on personal encouragement. But someone's got to do it. It is a question of visibility. Some of the opponents to women priests have very complex, unconscious reasons for it. The reasons are not always theological, and if they never see a woman preach or in the sanctuary it is very easy to hold fast to prejudice, but if they see it, it is a different matter. They can't say that I don't take liturgy seriously or mess it all up. The Anglican liturgy is very important to me and to them. And it is a lot harder to refuse communion from someone who has visited you, who has taken funerals and so on.' Alexandra does not see her role as proactively trying to change things so much as one of witness. It is very important to her to believe – and experience – that people do change: 'That has to be possible as Christians.'

Keeping faith: Celia's story (3)

Here we will pick up Celia's story where we left it: after her gruelling encounter with the responses of two clergy to her disastrous marriage, she decided to stand on her own two feet without the church. It was not until some years later, when one of her sons was attending confirmation classes at school, that she began to think about attending church again. Although this continues to be a deeply personal account, it will have resonances for a great many people – men and women – who have been drawn by the church into spiritual depth and felt the stirrings, in a broad sense, of vocation, not just to ordination, but to some sort of life in Christ.

Some years after she was excommunicated by Father X, her parish priest – years in which Father Y, who had behaved so importunately, had been involved in other scandals – Celia wrote to her local bishop. He visited her, listened sympathetically to her story, and wrote her a letter welcoming her back into the church. Her son was confirmed, and Celia became once more a regular churchgoer. As the years went on, and the children were beginning to leave home, she began to attend Bible study classes at the church. She also re-met an old friend, now a widower, who eventually asked her to marry him. He was not a churchgoer, and, his parents being agnostic, he had not been baptised. Nevertheless, they both felt they would like a church wedding, and that 'there was something redemptive and regenerative in this'. This took place, and was a very happy occasion with many family and friends; thereafter Celia and her husband regularly attended church together.

So far this is indeed a redemptive story, and that quality grew and continued over several years. Celia had been heard sensitively by the church authorities and had been granted a fresh start. She and her husband – even though she was divorced and he was not baptised – had received the grace of a church wedding. They were part of what turned out to be a revitalised community, joining in the choir, discussion groups, church cleaning, and so on, and making friends.

In due course Celia's husband, now aged fifty, said that he would like to be baptised and 'see where it led'. 'He was eventually very surprised', remarked Celia, 'to find that it led to his being baptised, confirmed and receiving his first communion all on the same evening! I was very proud to be his sponsor.' It was on the advice of their vicar, whom 'I respected, and respect as a very sensible and able priest (definitely a 'good' clergyperson!),' that Celia then began to explore the possibility of finding some ministry within the church, and she spent five 'very happy' years studying theology at a Roman Catholic college. Meanwhile, the ordination of women was moving closer to becoming a reality in the Anglican Church, there was a local shortage of clergy, and there was a need for volunteers to train as non-stipendiary ministers. Celia and her husband volunteered together: 'We both had this rather rosy (and naive!) picture of a husband-and-wife ministry which could include sharing with others some of the great redemptive happiness that we had found in our own second chance of life together in the church.'

Around this time, they joined a pilgrimage to the Holy Land led by their vicar, and this left on Celia 'a profound impression of how the church *could* be ... It brought home the simplicity of the church's early beginnings, stripped of all the accretions of later pomp and power.' It was also an important spiritual experience when they visited the well of the woman of Samaria (John 4:7), and she was asked to lower the bucket into the well – 'It seemed like a sign'. At the end of the pilgrimage the vicar invited her to give a short homily during a service at dusk in the garden where they were staying: 'I spoke without fear and with a great feeling of freedom and lightness of being, feeling, as it were, outside of myself, and that what I was doing was right.'

Soon after their return a newly ordained deacon, a woman, was appointed to the parish and there followed a number of unsatisfactory incidents. Celia had been involved in co-ordinating parish visiting, but the new deacon insisted that this was her domain. 'Perhaps,' remarked Celia, 'she felt insecure in a parish where we all knew each other so well' – and this is certainly an interpretation that makes sense. Nevertheless, the deacon seems to have introduced an element of rivalry which extended, for example, to deliberately refraining from telling Celia a parishioner had died, so that she met his widow unaware. She also objected to Celia having joined the team of servers, and appealed to the vicar for support. He visited Celia and her husband and asked them to curtail their activities, suggesting that, as a husband-and-wife team, they represented a 'power group'.

It was from this time onwards that Celia's path through church life 'went downhill'. Her husband was accepted for training as a non-stipendiary minister, and the vicar, who had previously encouraged Celia in her sense of vocation, and had invited her to preach during the pilgrimage, 'was now focusing on his future ordination and was withdrawing his support from mine'. There followed one of those events where a member of the church finds the attitudes of the church simply incomprehensible – not in the sense of not respecting that there are certain rules and boundaries, but in the way in which church officials display a supreme lack of tact in applying them. They were visited by a woman responsible for vetting candidates for ordination: she was 'courteous and brisk, and said that it was fortunate [sic] that Celia's husband's first wife had killed herself (rather than his being divorced) as this gave him the freedom to be ordained. She explained that the church did not countenance ordination of a remarried spouse with a former partner still living, so my ordination was out of the question.'

Celia was devastated, and no less so when the vicar, who was 'fundamentally a kind man', said that maybe it was just as well, since the fact that Celia's theological studies were taking place at a Roman Catholic college was 'suspect' and that she 'might have had trouble further down the line'. When she eventually received her diploma, after five years of study, she 'received no acknowledgement from the clergy or even a "well done" for a five-year slog' – just a blanket silence. The studies themselves had been immensely rewarding, but as Celia remarked '*Cui bono?* (Who benefits?)'. She describes the day of her husband's eventual ordination as 'the loneliest day of my life'. For the twelve years since their marriage, the church had been part of their life together: 'Now he was on the "inside" (part of the establishment) and I had returned to being an outsider.' She added, 'My customary response of "see if I care" failed me here!' She was keen to make it clear that her husband had in no way contributed to this feeling: 'I had encouraged him all the way, and with the advent of women's ordination I had said that this was enough to make me happy even if I had no part in it.'

When she asked the vicar what part he thought she should play in church life he said he thought that her role was to support her husband. 'I have tried to do this,' she said fifteen years later, 'not always successfully. It is one of the reasons I have not stopped going to church.' The other reasons are the people in the community and the good musical tradition, without which she might find it hard to keep going.

Some years after she had been turned down for ordination she asked a friend who had been ordained, but who was also divorced, how she had managed it. 'I didn't commit the cardinal sin of remarrying,' replied her friend with a grin. 'That is the problem.' What is very strange about this is that it is Celia's marriage that not only brought her husband into the church, but enables her to stay. It is a loving relationship in which, as she says, 'we release each other into freedom'. Again, for any ordinary person, the situation is hard to understand. Surely, one might say, this is a relationship in Christ: and yet it is this that stood in the way of her becoming a priest.

In spite of all this, Celia believes that 'the church is important in that it reminds us that we do not live in a totally secular world, and the church exists to carry on the teaching of the gospels. Good churches are good at this, and at their best, allow one to grow within them and to sit light to personal problems; to be able, like Brother Lawrence, to go about God's business – "and find it well performed".'[1]

Here then is someone who has managed to absorb repeated experiences of disillusionment and betrayal, and who – though aware of her own ambivalence – remains within the church and continues to believe in its function in society. She is one of those who dwell within the wounds of Christ's body, experiencing the pain and at the same time receiving the grace.

11

A gospel of encouragement

Whatever else church may be it is a coming together of people: you cannot really accept the Christian story and pay no attention to other people, even if your calling is essentially solitary, and this is something we can be glad about. We are social beings, and we thrive on good relationships. The positive side of 'the feel-good factor' is that we like to bond with other people, and when we do the effect can be to strengthen and encourage us. Our tendency to join the mob – any mob – is a distortion of our natural impulse to receive and provide encouragement, which is so much a part of church life when it is functioning well. We have seen how individuals and communities attract other people into the church, and how, in Jill's words, 'When you are connected with a group of people, you encourage each other.' Celia, although she supports her husband, is also encouraged by his constant support of her. Although the church has ordained him and not her, he has not sided with the church as an insider, while she remains an outsider: he brings her with him. Wanting to support him is, she says, one of the reasons she has not stopped going to church, but she also sings in the choir, and enjoys the friends they have in the church and in the parish generally. She is aware, however, that her parish is an exceptional one and, she says, 'were I not a member of this parish, I would probably not be going to church at all'.

Teresa talked of the tremendous encouragement she received when her husband had a long stay in hospital, and both parishioners and her parish priest visited him: 'I cannot tell you', she said, 'what a godsend that was, because I was under such pressure with work and visiting hours. I would walk in and see someone from church – the relief that would give me, to know that someone cared enough to spend a little time with him.'

We have also seen how the church itself, in its going on being, can act as encouragement, as a reminder that God loves us. A hospital chaplain spoke of how much she values the opportunity to be a witness to believing in something – simply the fact that she 'wears funny clothes' is, she feels, a potential encouragement to patients, a sign that there is something beyond the immediate experience of illness and death that surrounds them. In some ways she finds this more fulfilling than parish work, because, as she said, 'in a parish you are all taken up with your own maintenance'. As a chaplain she is able to take the gospel story out into the world, simply by being a Christian priest in a secular context. On the other hand, not being part of a parish means that she does not have the liturgical nourishment that a praying community provides, and she misses this terribly.

Another priest, a Roman Catholic, spoke of the spiritual encouragement he receives from the daily Mass at his church: 'It is one of the great bonuses of parish life. We have between fifteen and thirty-five people each morning and it is the bedrock of our worship. It feeds the Sunday liturgy, and our spiritual life revolves around that.'

The Gospel: a story of encouragement

The gospel story itself is run through with the importance of mutual encouragement. It is a story of fidelity, of bringing people into a loving relationship with God, not a story of a God who wants to condemn. As Alexandra put it: 'It is ridiculous to say that if you are not a Christian you are not saved. It is hard to believe in a God who is extremely interested in me in a loving and intimate way and then the moment I die there is a snap judgement. It is odd, and fickle and not at all God-like. I don't know what happens when I die, but I think the Gospel is good for me and good for the world.'

Christ himself is not some remote super-being, but relies throughout his ministry on his relationships – with human beings, with the Father, and also with the angels who minister to him, even if they are not commanded to intervene on his behalf. From the beginning of his ministry, Jesus gathers people around him, and these are not mere followers. Though he has a great deal to teach them and they are often slow to learn, his relationship with them is intimate and trusting. Finally, he says to them, 'I call you friends' (John 15:15). Friendship is something far more than mere discipleship. It is a relationship of equality and expresses mutual appreciation: not just our appreciation of God, but God's appreciation of us. At the same time, Jesus is constantly at one with the Father: 'Believe that I am in the Father and the Father in me' (John 14:11); and at the moment when he realises that even those closest to him will have to abandon him as he goes forward to trial and crucifixion, he says, ' "The hour is coming, indeed it has come, when you will be scattered, every man to his home and will leave me alone; Yet I am not alone, for the Father is with me" ' (John 16:32).

The encouragement inherent in the Gospel goes far deeper, however. The life of Christ is, as we have said, an immense act of solidarity between the Creator and the created. And in an act of ultimate encouragement, God not only follows our tragic destiny through to the bitter end – death – but also comes *through* death, overcoming death, because love is stronger than death.

Many of the resurrection texts of the Orthodox liturgy play with the idea that God cheated death, beat him at his own game. Hades is gleeful to see another corpse coming his way – and then horrified to discover who it is:

> *Today hell groans and cries aloud: 'My power has been destroyed. I accepted a mortal man as one of the dead: yet I cannot keep him prisoner, and with him I shall lose all those over whom I ruled. I held in my power the dead from all the ages; but see he is raising them all.'*[1]

The fact that Christ has overcome death does not of course mean that people no longer suffer or die. This continues. But death has been shown to be less effective than love itself. When Peter said to Christ, 'You have the words of eternal life', he surely meant something more complex than 'If we listen to you we will live for ever'. If we are honest most of us have very little idea of what eternal life could possibly mean, but most of us can relate to the idea of being part of something where death and destruction have finally given way to love. Claire described what this meant to her personally: 'We believe that Christ physically rose, and I believe in eternal life though I have no idea what form it will take. But what we are shown in the resurrection of Christ – when he comes back, but not for ever – is that we have to start understanding ourselves differently. It is a blueprint for the world to come. People who have died – especially those who have died in painful circumstances – we will be able to talk to them again and it will be all right. N. [a friend] was so self-destructive – he wasted his life – but there will be a world where he has not destroyed himself. Perfect love and perfect sacrifice free us all up. It is very complicated, but very important.'

The Christian story does not, of course, end with the resurrection of Christ, or even with the ascension, when redeemed humanity, the human person who has come through death, is taken into heaven. This would indeed leave us comfortless. But with Pentecost, as a token of redemption, Christ sends us the Spirit, the Comforter, the Encourager.

'No one lives alone any more': the coming of the Spirit

So far our theological reflection has focused almost exclusively on the church as the Body of Christ, but it is with Pentecost that the church becomes truly church, and the church, according to Maximos the Confessor, is like this:

> Men, women and children, all quite different from one another in birth, in size in nationality and language, in style of living and age, in trades and opinions, in clothes and customs and knowledge and rank, in welfare and appearance – all these are in the self same Church, all are reborn, newly created in the Spirit. No-one lives alone any more, but all are mutually joined together as brothers and sisters in the simple and indivisible power of faith.[2]

No one lives alone any more. This is our great gift and our great problem. As we have seen, each of us brings to this not-aloneness a personal history, and this personal history interacts with the church in ways which can nourish us or starve us, which can be redemptive or destructive, which can make the church essential in our lives or something to be avoided at all costs. In reflecting on our stories and our personal relationships within and with the church, we can discover the points at which church acquires a unique significance for each one of us; and we can also begin to glimpse what belongs to all of us, how our stories meet in the life of the Spirit.

How might this relate to our personal experience? One analogy is that of personal loss: the way in which through separations, and the ultimate experience of loss through death, we learn the deeper dimensions of relationships that transcend boundaries of time and space, not in any way undoing the reality of death or the agony of separation, but teaching us at first hand about a level of relationship that does not end even with death. Praying for the dead is, at the very least, an ongoing remembrance of that person, but just as the Eucharist is more than a mere memorial of the Last Supper, it is a coming together here and now in the invocation of the Spirit, so prayer for the dead is an ongoing relationship of understanding, of forgiveness, of growing closer together in God's love. Kate, who was harshly punished as a child, both loved her father and was very angry with him, and she struggled with this many years after he died: 'At first I did not know how to pray for him, because I did not know what that could mean: was I more compassionate than God? Did God need telling to be kind to him? But over the years, especially as I became older than he had been when I was a child, and was myself a mother, I began to sense his fragility, and how his desperate need to control us was part of that. Of course, you can say that is just my own internal process, but it certainly feels like more than that. I came to know him in a new way, and part of it was a real sense that he was now in the presence of love. It would be possible for him to be truly himself somehow.'

The searching out of the Spirit is something *we* need, not God. Finding ourselves exposed we naturally tend to hide (like Adam in the garden) or retaliate, or identify with a position of woundedness which means we do not have to make the effort to be healed: we become so impotent that we don't even reach out to touch the hem of the garment. Yet we are not loved because we are good: we hope to become good because we are loved.

Even in theology, however, the Spirit is elusive. The Spirit exists in the worship and sacraments of the church, and in writings on prayer and asceticism, long before there is any clear doctrine of who or what the Spirit is. Indeed, the doctrine of the Spirit followed on from worship. If the Spirit received the honour due to God, then the Spirit *was* God, not the other way round. It often seems easier to talk about the Spirit in an experiential way, in terms of what we sense, or experience, than to define what we mean by the person of the Spirit. Yet from the very beginning the coming of the Spirit is clearly bound up with our salvation, with the incarnation, death, resurrection and ascension of Christ. The Spirit descends at the Annunciation; the Spirit is promised at the ascension. The presence of the Spirit among us is the living church, church as Kingdom: 'Where the Church is there is the Spirit of God, and where the Spirit of God is, there is the Church.'[3]

When we invoke the Spirit in the Eucharist, then, we are making present the whole story of Christ's incarnation, death and resurrection here and now. All of us who take part in the Eucharist bring to it not only ourselves but our relationships, our life situations, everything that adds up to who we are. As Claire and others have described, it enables us to move beyond consciousness to a place where we can allow the subtlety of the Spirit to be more powerful even than our ability to name and understand. This may involve taking risks with our own understandings of who we are or might be, and is therefore something that is not easily undertaken by human beings. Trust is particularly difficult to cultivate perhaps in our rationalist age where we reckon to be able to understand and regulate most things, even death itself.

On the other hand, Alfred Hitchcock, the film director and master of suspense, said in an interview that he thanked heaven daily that 'tomorrow does not belong to any man. It belongs to God.'[4] Uncertainty about the future, he said, is one of God's most merciful and exciting gifts. Because of it, we can cultivate hope. The very elusiveness of the Spirit may teach us that we need not be afraid to have our assumptions questioned, even sometimes overturned. It is in *un*certainty that we develop a creative relationship to our faith. It often takes a 'throwing off balance' to persuade us to do that. The difficulty then is how we keep ourselves susceptible to that kind of subversion: retain the awareness, as Maximos the Confessor says, that 'our very being is on loan' to us.[5]

The church that I'd like

Perhaps then, church members and church authorities can be encouraged by the comments from some of our witnesses who have a strong sense that the spiritual and physical resources of the church are under-used. When churchgoers themselves are asked what they would like to see in the churches, their comments generate questions that perhaps help us to think about how to be church, to be the Body of Christ in this world, holding all the various dimensions shown in our 'map' of the body.

Does the church – itself filled with the Spirit – fill us with a sense of spiritual renewal?

There is a longing for the spiritual life of the church to be renewed. As one person put it, 'There is tremendous sadness about a person who has been a churchgoer all their life and never really stretched out to God in a growing kind of way.' We easily give way to habit, and forget that what we believe is an everyday reality. 'We believe in incarnation, in resurrection,' said Alexandra, 'and this has to talk to our living as well as our dying. The focus of our church should be now, rather than biding time or doing the right thing to get to heaven. This is it. We should make more of church here and now.'

The lack of spiritual vitality is, of course, partly a matter of the time and energy that is taken up in maintaining church life. Brenda, an Anglican priest who is now retired, values the opportunity to concentrate on being, rather than doing. 'Being who I am enables conversation,' she said. 'I am on the edge, and able to take time, and engage with what is happening in the world.' When she was involved in parish work she was, she feels, caught up in doing – in 'church politics, rotas, preaching, and the role'. All this took over from the essential role of being a priest, which for her begins with prayer.

Some people feel that the spiritual life is squashed by something even more fundamental, by the whole project of trying to be a religious institution. It is often said that eating together, making music together, going for a walk in the country and so on is a more liturgical experience than anything that goes on in church. As Michael put it, 'the religious purpose' can get in the way of any kind of spontaneous spiritual response.

Is worship something that deepens and widens our experience of God?

Our responses to worship often, of course, have as much to do with our own history and state of receptivity as with what is actually going on. People coming away from the same service, the same church community, will give very different impressions of what they have witnessed. The same parish which seems warm and welcoming to one can seem cold and exclusive to another. The service which for one person was full of dignity and prayerfulness will strike another as empty show – 'God-bothering'. One person will be deeply moved by the same hymns which to another are sentimental trash.

Nevertheless, all the churches have a great wealth of resources that are barely known to the average member, let alone used. Our liturgy draws not only on the last two thousand years but on the whole Jewish tradition as well. There are immense riches both in terms of understanding what it is we believe, and how we might reflect on that, and also in the living connection of shared prayer across the centuries. Yet many people feel that liturgy fails to come alive. 'What the church desperately needs is spiritual renewal,' said one Catholic woman, 'and the Vatican is contributing nothing to this.' She felt she had to look hard for the mystical element even in liturgy, and this is a common problem for all the churches: 'There doesn't seem much room for surprise in the churches,' said Michael. 'It is all very mundane.' Even where liturgical practice has been carefully preserved, as in the Orthodox Church, unless it is celebrated with a transparency that looks beyond itself, it too can become merely a pageant, a curiosity.

There, is of course, and always will be, a huge tension between preserving the liturgical traditions while at the same time being open to people here and now. As will no doubt already be clear, I love and value traditional liturgy and church music, and find immense depth in it. We lose it at our peril. At the same time, I have become painfully aware of how even liturgy itself can become an obsession. Fights break out over whether some detail of liturgical practice should be done one way or another way, and I know only too well how powerful the feelings involved can be, especially if there are different understandings of what these practices mean.

For example, in some Orthodox churches it is still the practice, as it was in the West not so long ago, to say all the prayers at the heart of the liturgy secretly in the sanctuary while the choir sings. To me personally this seems to make a mockery of the dialogue between priest and people that leads up to the invocation of the Spirit on the bread and wine, and if my first experience of Orthodoxy had been in a church where this was obscured, I doubt if I ever would have become a member. For others, however, it expresses something quite different. The priest has been sent into the sanctuary to make this offering on our behalf, and prayer is going on in the church at many different levels, of which the singing of the choir is one. For such a person, not only is their participation in the liturgy just as complete whether or not they hear these prayers, but it would be quite shocking to have them said aloud for the congregation to hear.

It is essential that we learn to listen to each other about what different practices mean rather than simply cling to them, or become impatient and throw them out. An organist with a very well-trained choir complained that the vicar had tried to impose Taizé singing on them. 'It is very dull for a trained choir,' he said, 'and she was unable to comprehend how singers approach a service.' The Taizé singing continued to be part of the services, and to arouse great resentment in the choir who felt it was foisted on them. It was not until a *locum tenens* priest came into the situation that the problem was resolved. 'He took time to get to know the choir and what mattered to them about the singing. And he was able to explain what was valuable about Taizé as well,' said the organist. Though not, perhaps, converted, he could see how people were drawn in to the meditative quality of the chant.

As with anything we love, we can lose sight of the true nature of liturgy, and its various components, by caring too passionately about it so that it becomes an end in itself. There is also the difficulty that it takes time to enter into liturgical experience. By stripping down liturgy to the essentials and doing away with what some people see as 'public display', we may indeed do away with off-putting and distracting material; in the process, however, we may lose something that, given time, allows us to move ever more deeply into relationship with God, with each other and with human beings at large, alive and dead. How any of the churches maintain the depth of the tradition without allowing it to fossilise is one of the greatest challenges: there is a tension between tradition and the newness that has to be part of our everyday experience of church.

This was something that confronted a retired Anglican priest, steeped in liturgical tradition, who was invited by her local parish to take part in an anointing service. She readily accepted, only to experience something like horror in her traditionalist heart when the vicar told her: 'I've added glitter to the chrism because there are so many children here.' Nevertheless, somewhat against her inclinations, she proceeded to take part in the ceremony since it would have been churlish to do otherwise. The effect, she had to admit afterwards, was stunning. Only a few weeks before people had been marked on their foreheads on Ash Wednesday, and had walked out of church anointed with this visible darkness. And now these same people, and many children, were walking out of church not just with their foreheads glistening with oil, but shining with the glitter. 'It was a real image of the joyfulness of the resurrection,' she remarked, amused at her own surprise.

How do our church buildings function in the community?

One Good Friday some years ago, we were preparing our church for the afternoon service which centres on the burial of Christ. A structure representing the tomb is decorated with flowers and the icon of Christ laid within it. A man who walked by remarked on how we as a community made the church into a home, and this was true. There was a very real sense in which we all shared personally in the building in which we prayed and celebrated the liturgy together. At the same time we were – and still are – aware that it could be much more. We have not yet found a way of doing it, but it seems a terrible waste that this place of prayer should be locked up except when there is a service.

People and traditions differ, of course, on the question of whether church buildings should be simply houses of prayer or be available for all kinds of other functions. Not everyone is as extreme as Liz, our radical priest from Chapter 7, who pointed out that Christ did not command us to 'meet together in large outdated buildings'. The churches, she feels, are failing to incarnate Christ in the world because they concentrate so much on worship and so little on people's needs. 'We need to feed people before we talk about prayer,' she said. 'We should be funding people not buildings. The whole church structure is unnecessarily expensive.' She would like to see all the buildings sold, and the money used to fund a community facility staffed with psychologists, advisers, play therapists and so on. Services could take place in other institutions, such as schools out of hours. 'The problems of the average family are not about God, or prayer, but about work, money, illness – what is the church doing? We have got to get back to Jesus – what did he spend his time doing?'

Others, while less radical, would like to see more use made of church buildings for the community. As one man said, 'There is a wealth of buildings and the community is locked out of them for most of the year. People are just too precious about keeping the insides just so.' Another said, 'Church buildings should be open, beautiful places. They should be used for groups, for meals, be part of the community.' Even if churches are kept simply for prayer and worship, this in itself is a valuable resource, providing they are accessible in some way. An Anglican church in my area, although kept locked, keeps open a small enclave from which it is possible to see into the church to where the sacrament is reserved. This always seems to me a genuine and valuable attempt at hospitality. There are also, of course, many churches, particularly in cities, which either stay open or hold services that people can attend before or after work and in their lunch hours, and this too is a very important gift to the surrounding society, and much valued by those who make use of it.

Are we witnessing to the Gospel in society at large?

Alan, an adult convert to Christianity, is 'very unhappy' about what he sees as a general hardening of attitudes in the churches. 'I would like to see us being more vulnerable in daily life,' he said. 'The church is no longer a beacon of civilisation, and this is a good thing. We can concentrate on our social and spiritual responsibilities: identify social need and be a thorn in the flesh of society.' For John, too, the loss of status in society that the church has suffered is a great (and under-exploited) opportunity for social and political action: 'I like the idea that we are in a minority,' he said. 'There is nothing automatic about it. It almost raises the status of belief.' One of the things that has taken him (pleasantly) by surprise as a church member is that the churches are not afraid of getting involved in political controversy and protest, for example about Third World debt. By contrast, however, he added, 'a lot of churches spend a lot of time asking for money for themselves. The money is necessary for them to keep going, but I wish it were otherwise.'

John's thoughts were echoed by Claire who, like many Anglicans, would like to see the Anglican Church disestablished so that it could be more radical, 'a thorn in the side, as it was always intended to be'. She would also like to see Christians make a real attempt to live more simply, for those with money to give it, and for ritual to be stripped down so that it does not distract us from the message of love. 'If we all try to love properly,' she remarked, 'who knows what we could achieve in this world.'

Claire feels strongly that churches can be powerful forces for good. 'If you jettison religion, you get rid of one line of morality. For example the way people resist tyranny often emerges from the best of religious tradition.'

The churches also have vast theological resources for speaking out on green issues, and this again is something their members would like see more of. 'It's a matter of standing up and talking about what we believe,' said one young woman. 'The churches do have the power to change how people behave at both the social and the personal level.'

Many church members, of course, are struggling simply to survive and find time to worship as well. 'I would like to see the parishioners be more self-aware about their involvement in the wider community,' said a Catholic priest. 'None of them volunteer for things.' This was in his view largely a question of time and resources. 'What I would really like is for people to be less harassed,' he said, 'so that there would be more time to work for justice and peace.'

Are we ourselves living out a gospel of love and encouragement?

To be a living body in the world in which we live, to be one that is receptive to the Spirit, we need to find in each other the courage to face the concerns of the people around us, including those of gender and sexuality, the family, medical science and so on. In doing so we need to allow ourselves to be nourished and liberated, not suffocated, by our tradition.

The desire that the church should live out a gospel of love – and encouragement – comes up again and again in talking with people. 'The message we should be getting across', said Margaret, 'is that human beings are wonderful, but they are even better alongside the Creator. It is not a guilt-inducing message – "I am pious and you are not" – but encouraging people to be themselves.' As another person put it, 'The people who are most prepared to go out and connect with the outside world are not necessarily the best people to do that: they just put people off.' She spoke of a Good Friday procession in her local shopping centre where a Christian group were standing with 'huge purple banners'. She felt all this did was to give other people the message that they were meant to feel guilty. 'It just feeds people's prejudices,' she said. 'Why can't they go out on Easter Day with yellow banners for the resurrection instead?'

A recurring theme is a perceived gap between the Gospel and the attitudes of the church, particularly when it comes to attitudes to women and to sexual orientation. While there are clearly many other things that do and should concern us in being church, these are the areas in which people within the churches, as well as people outside them, principally find themselves unable to match what they read in the gospels to the attitudes of the churches themselves. To quote Celia: 'What the church in general appears not to be doing at the present moment is addressing the scandal of its hierarchical structure, its attitude to women or those of different sexual orientation or other minority groups. It should not be in the business of keeping out but of drawing in.' Celia, as we know, values the support and friendship of her local church community, but the gap between local church fellowship and the behaviour and attitudes of the institution at large is a problem.

Likewise Teresa, who, as we saw in Chapter 2, has a Catholic education and liturgical experience deeply engraved in her heart, grieves over what she calls 'the unloving aspects of the church', on a number of issues, even though much of her personal experience has been of caring communities and individuals. The Catholic Church, she feels, 'could do with some female priests: I've had too many hard-line male educators and priests.' All this is part of wanting the Catholic Church to 'be more human'. And she is scandalised by the church's stance on homosexuality. Like many others, she looks at her gay friends who share all the joys and sorrows of relationships in the same way that other people do, and is simply puzzled: 'We should be encouraging people to treat other people more lovingly, not pointing the finger. I have many gay friends, and I don't want them excluded any more than divorced people. I can't say it is unnatural to be gay: it is part of creation. We should be loving as a church and we are being unloving to a huge group of people. I agree with marrying gay couples in church – not as a political act, but as loving support for the couple.'

Both Celia's and Teresa's comments go to the heart of what is a problem for many people. The Gospel and their hearts tell them one thing, as does their experience of people they know: the church tells them another. This was the reason Frances left the church as we saw in Chapter 6. As Jeffrey put it, 'They need to get out of this them-and-us mentality. A lot of "them" are my friends and family.'

Margaret feels that individual Christians simply have to go ahead and try and live the Gospel as they perceive it, accepting that the church institutions themselves will never be able to reach a common position. 'When it comes to issues such as abortion and homosexuality,' she pointed out, 'the churches cannot take common action because there are so many different views – and attempts to reach common ground can lead to a hardening of attitudes. I'm not even sure if it is the role of the church as a whole, so much as of people who are Christian – it comes as a fruit of church membership.' Like so many others, she feels the churches are obsessed with sex, and in their pronouncements lose contact with the mutual respect and love which are at the heart of the Gospel.

'I just ignore all those bits, 'said Claire, 'it is just the church being silly, and I have not got time for it. They can only talk about what people do. They make sex hugely powerful and denigrate it at the same time. They can't talk about love. I'd like to see it all go.' She feels that the churches themselves are moving on regardless of what the authorities say: 'The battle over the ordination of women is won. Things will change for the Roman Catholics too. It is not possible to hold the anomalies, for example the married ex-Anglican priests being accepted when there are priests who have made a lifelong sacrifice in being celibate. And,' she added, 'people have had just about enough of celibates having illicit sex. Respect for the old order is going. Child protection is taken seriously. It is all getting more real.' This was her more optimistic view. On the other hand, she does not see the huge general growth in religion as encouraging: 'It will simply polarise people and harden attitudes, and it is very difficult to see a way ahead for people like me. The church as I understand it [i.e. the liberal church] may die.'

Alexandra, who, as we have seen in the previous chapter, has had her share of struggles as an Anglo-Catholic priest, is determined not to let this happen: 'I'm fond of the church. When I am angry and want to leave, as I am sometimes tempted to do, I think "Why should I leave it to people who make me cross?" It's my church as well as their church. We have to compromise if we are all going to have ownership: what is true for individuals has to be true for the church, even if it is grim.'

As divided churches, do we genuinely regret our inability to be united, or do we each simply claim a monopoly on the truth?

'Any Christian', said John, 'should be welcome in any service at any time. We should be able to walk through the doors of any church and always be welcomed whatever grievances may exist.' A pastoral assistant at a large city church described disunity, however, as 'the single biggest problem', adding, 'It is particularly difficult when a group of people believe that unless you believe exactly what they believe you are going to go to hell.' The quest for unity between the churches will not – and must not – go away, but perhaps we have to accept, given our human condition, that we will not achieve it. This does not mean, however, that any church needs to identify itself over against any other, or claim to be the one true church. How can any of the churches – the Orthodox, the Catholics, or anyone else – claim that, in the light of how we behave towards each other, towards our members and towards the world at large?

This surely does not mean that any of us should relativise what we believe or our own traditions. We should be drawing on them as deeply as possible: not in order to undermine or take over anyone else's, but in order to develop a depth of understanding that Christ is all in all, one that enables us to be open to what we can learn from perceiving Christ in each other. A common complaint is that clergy and laity cling too closely to what they believe and need to impose it on other people, rather than being so secure in what they believe that they can allow others to question and explore.

An image given to me by an Anglican priest has helped me in thinking about this. One day, when she was gathering stones on a beach, she realised that each of the stones had some kind of line across it. She arranged them in a circle in such a way that although the stones were all of different shapes, sizes and colours, the lines across them also formed a circle, complete but fragmented. She placed this circle at the intersection of some paving stones, which forms a cross behind them. The cross is unarguably there in the background, but the stones rest on the rock-like surface of the paving stone. The stones themselves are very individual, and the continuity of the lines making the circle is extremely tenuous. But it is there. It is an image of individuality, of difference, and of fragile unity that speaks to me of our condition as churches today. Surely our very difference – the variety of creation that is given by God himself – should not prevent us from agreeing to be church together, each contributing our own shape and size and colour to the circle? When we – separately – celebrate the Eucharist, each of us brings to that our story, our culture, our ways of thinking – a variety that no human being, and indeed no human institution, can ever expect to accommodate, though surely the gospels teach us that we should not give up on trying to expand our consciousness as far as we can.

© The Revd Dr Louise Adey Huish

The closest we can get to expressing this corporately is in the Eucharist, which, as has been suggested in Chapter 7, is the place where all these different aspects of the church as Body of Christ that people long to see visibly lived out intersect. It is also clear that we are simply incapable of achieving the unity – between each other, between ourselves and God, between God and all creation, seen and unseen – that the Eucharist expresses. There is a sense in which any celebration of the Eucharist is a complete expression of this. At the same time any celebration is inevitably partial in terms of the ability of any of us to participate in that. Only in Christ can there be 'all in all' – and when Christ is all in all we shall no longer need even the Eucharist. Meanwhile, it is important to continue to celebrate it, even if we can only do so in disunity, in order to let it work on us individually and corporately: it expresses something that already exists. As Cardinal Cormack Murphy O'Connor said when he celebrated Mass in York Minster for the four hundredth anniversary of Mary Ward (the first time the head of the Catholic Church had done this since the Reformation), 'Occasions like this show how important is the real communion that exists between the Anglican Church and ourselves.'[6]

That real communion does not go away. It is what one Catholic woman referred to when she said, 'If only the church could be spiritually radical, we could have a society that was all church.' That would require each and all of us to be so spiritually radical that we could be completely in touch with that pre-existing unity at every level, and of course this will never happen in this life. It is, however, an argument for the church continuing to be, and continuing to celebrate the Eucharist, incarnating it in this world, invoking the Spirit, and allowing all of us a personal – however partial – participation in it. To do this may involve not only accepting our limitations, but realising that an awareness of them might help us to be open rather than closed: such an awareness can make room for the Spirit to enter our individual and communal lives. Nowhere have I seen this better expressed than in the words of Leonard Cohen:

> Ring the bells that can still ring.
> Forget your perfect offering.
> There is a crack in everything.
> That's how the light gets in.[7]

Life in the cracks

As we have seen, many who stay within the church are only too aware that they inhabit a wounded body. My friend's circle of stones lying on the paving stone also speaks to me of the fact that the cross is built in to the world we inhabit. Crucifixion, and our propensity to crucify others, will not go away either within the church or outside it. Christ has, however, followed through the consequences of this, and overcome them. Thus the cross becomes not only something we have to bear but something that we are sustained by. The rock that is Christ will not desert us. The fragile circle of the lines made by the stones speaks to me of our connections with each other: of course the rock is visible in the chinks between the stones.

For me, as for a number of other people whose stories are included here, that connection is most visible in the monastic life which is as essential to the life of the churches as the more everyday manifestations. These are people who are often on the edge of both church and society, and are themselves struggling to understand what a monastic vocation means in our present age. They experience all the difficulties of living in community that anyone else does – and yet they keep going a quiet pulse of prayer, which is not only essential for the life of the churches, but also sustains many people who come in contact with them. For myself, coming to know communities and solitaries of various denominations, in a number of different ways, has been crucial in being able to hang on to the idea that going on being church is worthwhile.

It will be clear by now that my own path in the church has been far from smooth – for me or for my fellow members. Why am I still here? Nine days out of ten the answer is 'Because I haven't left yet'. What is the answer on the tenth day?

The tenth day answer has something to do with this book, and the people in it, and with honouring my own experience. In a Sunday sermon not long ago, a priest recommended to us that we remember our experiences in the church. They can sustain us, he said, when times are hard. Afterwards, he had the grace to smile when I commented that what he had said was true: 'I *am* sustained', I said, 'by remembering my experiences in the church – so long as I remember also that I survived them.' This was not altogether fair on my part. My own experiences of church are a microcosm of everything we find in this book. Within the church, I have been wonderfully nourished and supported, horribly betrayed, vilified and envied. As well as the bad times there have been marvellous, life-enhancing experiences, practical support and times of great depth and stillness; church has become for me an ongoing sense of deep connection in prayer with other people – not necessarily with people within my own church or my own community – but with many who, one way or another, continue to strive to be part of the Body of Christ. Father Alexander Schmemann, a theologian of the first-wave emigration from Russia put it like this:

> *The miracle of the Church assembly is that it is not the 'sum' of the sinful and unworthy people who comprise it, but the Body of Christ. How often do we say we are going to church to obtain help, strength, consolation? We forget meanwhile that we ARE the church, we make it up, that Christ abides in his members ... we are in Christ and Christ in us.*[8]

This is the inspiration: how it will work out in practice is another matter. The outlook is not encouraging, but as Hitchcock said, tomorrow belongs to God. Fortunately, it is not simply down to us, but if we really believe what we profess, we do have to be open to the unexpected.

It cannot be too strongly stressed that Jesus' disciples did not in any practical sense realise that there would be a resurrection after Christ was crucified. Like us, they were earthbound, wounded, not knowing where to turn. No more than the myrrh-bearing women on Easter morning, can we expect everything to come right. We can only go on doing what we can to keep love alive: not covering up, not pretending life is not as it is, but 'speaking the truth in love'. This is what it meant to go to the tomb on Easter morning to anoint the body of Jesus, paying it 'the gentlest attention'. They had no expectation that he would not be dead: they were doing what you do for a dead person you love. Only by practising whatever love we can manage, with whatever honesty we can manage, will we come to appreciate that the world we live in is truly loved by God: that the love is there for the taking.

We began this book with a quotation from Stacey MacAindra, the central character of Margaret Lawrence's novel, *The Fire Dwellers*. Stacey is married to a salesman for RICHALIFE vitamins, who is also the son of a retired minister. A depressed mother of four, she agonises every Sunday when her father-in-law calls round for lunch, about how she is going to explain to him that the children are gradually dropping out of Sunday school. Towards the end of the novel, she comes to realise that the husband she experiences as unbearably non-communicative bears his burdens alone. 'If he doesn't deal with everything alone, no help, then he thinks he's a total washout.' He got this from his father she reckons, but 'at least' she says to her father-in-law in her head, 'you had your heavenly Father to strengthen your right arm or resolve, to put the steel reinforcing in your spine. Mac's only got himself.' Her subsequent thought on church is that there is no quick fix – but for some people, something is given.[9]

Whatever the inadequacies of the church, they do not change the fact that God is trying to make that 'something' – that encouragement – available to us. The churches are well placed to hear and spread the message that it is so. Only time will tell whether, or to what extent, they are able to do so, but the message itself will not go away.

Notes

1 Putting the church on trial

1 A thought of the character Stacey MacAindra in Margaret Lawrence, *The Fire Dwellers* (McClelland and Stuart, 1969), p. 277.
2 David Lodge, *Thinks* (London: Penguin Books, 2002), p. 29.

2 To go or not to go – what draws us to church?

1 Augustine, *Confessions*, Book 1.
2 C. S. Lewis, *A Grief Observed* (London: Faber and Faber, 1961).
3 James MacMillan, 'In harmony with heaven', *The Tablet*, 11 October 2008, pp. 12–13.
4 Harry Williams CR (1910–2006).
5 H. A. Williams, *Some Day I'll Find You* (London: Mitchell Beazley, 1982).
6 The Revd Dr Vigo Auguste Demant (1893–1983), Canon of Christ Church, Oxford, and Professor of Moral and Pastoral Theology in Oxford University from 1949 to 1971.
7 Brother Lawrence (Nicholas Herman, c. 1605–91), *Practice of the Presence of God: The Best Rule of Holy Life* (London: Hodder & Stoughton, 1998; first published 1692). Nicholas Herman became Brother Lawrence at the age of 55 when he entered the Carmelite order in Paris as a lay brother. A distinctive feature of his writing is that he saw no distinction between 'the time of business' and 'the time of prayer'.
8 C. S. Lewis, *The Screwtape Letters* (London: Fount, 1988; first published 1942).

4 Witnesses for the defence

1 Matins Canon for Theophany (the Baptism of Christ). Canticle 6 in *The Festal Menaion*, tr. Mother Mary and Archmandrite Kallistos Ware (St Tikhon's Seminary Press, 1978), p. 373.
2 1 Kings 3
3 From the Marriage Service in the Book of Common Prayer.

5 Witnesses for the prosecution

1 One of many comments that emerged when people with HIV/AIDS were asked what they would like to say to pastors. Michael Séan Paterson, *Singing for Our Lives: Positively Gay and Christian* (Sheffield: Cairns Publications, 1997), p. 69.
2 'Inclusive Church' is an organisation founded in August 2003, committed to challenging exclusivity on the grounds of race, gender or sexuality. Its website is www.inclusivechurch2.net.
3 On 20 July 2007.

6 When the event is mightier than the structure

1 'Transferring the Untransferrable – a paradox linking poetry and psychosis, theology and therapy', Regents College, London, 1991.
2 Cf. Psalm 41:8.
3 See Fyodor Dostoevksy, *The Brothers Karamazov*, tr. R. Pevear and L. Volokhonsky (London: Vintage, 1992), p. 245.
4 A.-M. Rizutto, *The Birth of the Living God* (University of Chicago Press, 1981).
5 David Lodge, *Thinks* (London: Penguin Books, 2002), pp. 28ff.

7 What is it all for?

1 From J. Stevenson (ed.), *Creeds, Councils and Controversies* (London: SPCK, 1969), pp. 352–3. Even then, it has to be said, there were some who could not sign up to this, and to this day the mainstream Eastern Churches are not generally in communion with the non-Chalcedonians, though dialogue continues.
2 Prayer at the Great Blessing of the Waters, *The Festal Menaion*, p. 356.
3 From 'The Riddle of the Sparks', in Pamela Vermes, *The Riddle of the Sparks* (Oxford: Foxcombe Press, 1993), pp. 11–22. Quoted by kind permission of Professor Geza Vermes.
4 From the same prayer at the Blessing of the Waters.
5 Canticle Four of the Matins Canon in Tone 2 (Octoechos translated by the Orthodox Monastery of the Protecting Veil of the Mother of God, Bussy-en-Othe, France).

8 The body broken

1 Mother Mary Agnes, the founder of the community, has written four autobiographical books describing her journey, all published by SPCK, the most recent in 2003: *A Tide that Sings*, *The Song of the Lark*, *Island Song* and *For Love Alone*.
2 Jenny Gaffin, 'The Bumbling Pastoral Worker', *Practical Theology*, vol. 1:3, February 2009.
3 Jonathan Sacks, *The Home We Build Together: Recreating Society* (London: Continuum, 2007), p. 149.

NOTES   189

4 I owe this phrase to a sermon preached by Bishop Basil of Amphipolis for the Sunday of the myrrh-bearers in May 2008: 'Something that requires our gentlest attention', available on the internet at www.exarchate-uk.org/Bishop_Basil/BBsermons/2008_Myrrhbearers.html.

9 The problem of the 'feel-good factor'

1 'A Good Man is Hard to Find' in Flannery O'Connor, *A Good Man is Hard to Find* (London: Women's Press, 1980), p. 28.
2 A verse, usually omitted now, from the hymn 'All things bright and beautiful'.
3 http://www.guardian.co.uk/commentisfree/2008/jun/20/transport.religion.
4 O'Connor, *A Good Man is Hard to Find*, p. 28.
5 Olivier Clément, *The Roots of Christian Mysticism* (Hyde Park, NY: New City Press, 1993), p. 49. Maximos (*c.* 580–662) is known as 'the Confessor' because he held out against the church authorities insisting that Christ had both a human and a divine will instead of a single divine will – otherwise it could not be said that he was fully human. He was condemned for heresy, and, though already in his eighties, his tongue was cut out, his right hand was cut off, and he was sent into exile. Twenty years after his death they realised he had been right, and he was declared a doctor of the church.
6 Matthew 5:3–11.

10 Living within the wounds of Christ's body

1 See Chapter 2, note 7.

11 A gospel of encouragement

1 Stichera on 'Lord, I have cried ...', Vespers of Holy Saturday in the Orthodox rite. *The Lenten Triodion*, tr. Mother Mary and Archimandrite Kallistos Ware (South Canaan, PA: St Tikhon's Deminary Press, 2001) p. 656.
2 Maximus the Confessor, *Mystogogia*, 1 (PG91, 664), quoted in Thomas Spidlik (ed.), *Drinking from the Hidden Fountain: A Patristic Breviary* (London: New City, 1992), pp. 319–20.
3 Irenaeus of Lyon *Against* Heresies III.38.1, in J. Stevenson (ed.), *A New Eusebius: Documents Illustrating the History of the Church to AD 337*, new edn rev. W. H. C. Frend (London: SPCK, 1987), p. 113.
4 'Would you like to know your Future?' in *Hitchcock on Hitchcock*, ed. S. Gottlieb (Berkeley: University of California Press, 1995).
5 In Maximos the Confessor, 'Commentary on the Lord's Prayer', in *The Philokalia*, tr. G. E. H. Palmer, P. Sherrard and K. Ware (London: Faber and Faber, 1990), p. 297.
6 *Sunday*, BBC Radio 4, 1 February 2008.
7 The refrain to Cohen's song, 'Anthem'.
8 A. Schmemann, *The Eucharist: Sacrament of the Kingdom*, tr. Paul Kachur (Crestwood, NY: St Vladimir's Seminary Press, 1988), p. 23.
9 Lawrence, *The Fire Dwellers*, p. 257.

Index

Proper names in quotation marks refer to interviewees

Abortion 89, 178
'Alan' 108, 176
'Alexandra' 159, 166, 171, 179
'Alice' 105, 106
Anger 64, 154, 155, 156
Anglican Church (16, 21, 32, 73, 86, 87, 130, 131, 161, 176, 182; *see also* Church of England
Anglican Communion 35, 88
Anglicanism 7, 32
'Anna' 107
Annulment (of marriage) 122
Antidoron 131
Apostles 44, 83, 97
Art 1, 14, 156
Articles of Faith 21
Atheist Bus Campaign 145
Atonement 16
Authority 127, 153
'Avril' 154

Beatitudes 147
Bereavement 17, 18, 80, 153
'Beverley' 24
Body of Christ 2, 4, 5, 43, 60, 64, 110, 113, 116, 139, 171, 181, 184
Boredom 63
'Brenda' 66, 69, 171
Building (church) 3, 14, 21, 51, 63, 107, 127, 174ff

Catholic Church 21, 22, 35, 87, 88, 120, 121, 178, 182; and divorce 96
'Celia' 26ff, 94ff, 140, 160ff, 165, 177f
Chalcedon, Council of 110
Chaplain(s) 25, 39, 51, 56, 69, 131, 132, 166
Child protection 179
Choir 15, 16, 19, 21, 26, 29, 31, 48, 70, 74, 100, 106, 115, 140f, 157, 160, 165,173
Christianity 1, 16, 25, 66, 78, 89, 114, 134; inseparable from church 109
Church of England 24, 81, 131; *see also* Anglican Church

Church of Scotland 11, 125
'Claire' 23, 46, 53, 109, 140, 147, 168, 170, 176, 179
Cohen, Leonard 182
Communion 6, 19, 24, 37, 57, 81, 88, 89, 91, 96, 102, 105, 116, 119, 122–3, 182; Christmas 14; 'dual integrity' 87, 159; exclusion from 120f, 157; first 161; forgiveness 46; open policy 130f; rifts in 80, 124ff; with God 19
Community 6, 11, 12, 14, 19, 23, 24, 29ff, 34, 47f, 50, 51, 64, 86, 89, 126, 124, 127, 132, 152f, 163, 166, 172, 183; boundaries of 92; Christ-centred 4; clergy role 75; faith 1, 2; lack of generosity 70; support 58f
Confession 28, 95, 105, 123
Confirmation 26, 28, 160; classes 22, 27
Conflict; in community 47, 64f, 86; internal 86, 96, 157
Conversion 81
Covenant 134
Cox, Murray 85
Creed 17, 109
Crowd mentality 144
Crucifixion 5, 97, 144, 146, 147, 167, 182
Culture 5, 32, 33, 35, 48, 88f, 134, 181

Death 6, 18, 60, 63, 64, 133, 145, 146, 155, 167f, 169; of Jesus 139, 170
Denant, Canon 26
Depression 89, 155
Desire 13, 14, 15, 30, 140
Discipleship 140f, 167
Disestablishment 176
Division 112, 120, 123, 125, 128, 132
Divorce 32, 96, 120, 121, 122

Ecclesiology 60
Ecumenical Patriarchate 126–7, 128
'Ellen' 66
Envy 142, 143, 152
Eternal life 167
Eucharist 2, 6, 16, 36, 55, 56, 57, 60, 87,

106, 115f, 124, 126, 128, 135, 140, 169, 170, 181; Anglican 119; focus of unity 120; incarnational 114; space for forgiveness 46
Evensong 24, 30
Exclusion 133
Exile 15, 34

Faith 1, 2, 14, 15, 17ff, 63, 68, 71, 92, 134, 149; beacon of hope 23; crisis of 59, 119; keeping 160; personal 30; putting into practice 107f; unquestioning 27
Fall, the 18
Family 13, 15, 18, 25, 26, 56, 76, 94, 101, 152, 178; church as 12, 32; extended 60; Holy 52; influence 21, 23; service 47; time for 72f
Finnes, John 19
Football 3, 105
Forgiveness 45, 46, 69, 148, 154, 155
'Frances' 18f, 25, 80ff, 88ff, 109
'Fred' 88
Freud, Sigmund 155
Friends 23, 160, 165, 167, 178
Friendship 16, 167
Fundamentalists 132
Funerals 6, 55, 56, 126, 159

Gaffin, Jenny 133
Gaudi, Antoni 52
Generosity 70f, 143
'George' 87, 102
Gethsemane 146
Ghandi, Mahatma 113
Grace 53, 163; cheap 154
Green issues 176
Guilt 13, 97, 147, 177

Healing 139, 148
Heaven 6, 141, 170
Hell 78, 167, 180
Heresy 68, 127
Herod 43
Hitchcock, Alfred 170, 184
Holiness 66, 74
Holy Spirit *see* Spirit
Hope 23, 54, 69, 98, 99, 100
Hospitality 36ff, 175; of Abraham and Sarah 37f

Imitation 140f

Incarnation 2, 109f, 114, 135, 148, 170, 171
'Inclusive Church' 79

'James' 32, 80
'Jane' 17, 65
'Jeffrey' 68, 70, 90ff, 110
Jesus 43, 44, 45, 49, 68, 79, 97f, 107, 110, 135, 139, 141, 143, 144, 145, 146, 147, 148, 158, 166, 184
'Jill' 57ff, 140, 141, 152, 165
'John' 19, 45f, 70f, 106f, 116, 176, 179
John the Baptist 44f
Judas 97f, 143, 158
Julian of Norwich 17

Karamazov, Ivan 99
'Kate' 146, 169
'Kevin' 155

Lawrence, Brother 26, 163
Lewis, C.S. 18, 26
LGCM 102
Liturgy 7, 16, 19, 33, 34, 48, 60, 66, 70, 79, 81, 88, 109, 111, 119, 126, 129, 131, 159, 166, 167, 172ff, 175
Liturgical cycle 49f, 94
'Liz' 175f
Lodge, David 2, 101
Logos 111
Lynch, Rev Bernard 133

'Margaret' 21, 177, 178
Marriage 12, 21, 58, 95, 96, 122, 153, 160, 163; break-up 32
'Mark' 55
'Mary' 116, 122f, 126
Mary, Mother of God 24, 49
Mass 28, 79, 87, 101, 116, 120, 123, 131, 157, 166
Maximos the Confessor 146, 168, 171
McMillan, James 20
'Meg' 30
Melangell, Saint 54
Methodist Church 30
'Michael' 22, 31, 76f, 108, 113, 134, 158, 172
Money 69, 98
Music 1, 3, 14, 15, 16, 20, 21, 22, 25, 33, 45, 50, 56, 105, 107, 140, 159, 172f
Myrrh-bearing women 69, 98
Mystical experience 13, 60, 105–6

Natural law 111
Need(s) 4, 13, 175

O'Connor, Cardinal Cormac Murphy 182
O'Connor, Flannery 143, 145
Orthodox Church 7, 16, 33, 35, 36, 48, 79, 88, 89, 90, 120, 129, 172

Parable of Talents 132
Parish Council 34, 69, 79, 158
Part-time work 72f
Pastoral care 16, 86, 95, 113, 115, 152
Pentecost 133, 168
Pilate, Pontius 43
Politics 7, 12, 171
Power 27, 162; of Spirit 28
Positive ecumenism 132
Prayer 1, 17, 20, 30, 36, 54, 60, 64, 83, 86, 91, 93, 102, 115, 116, 140, 142, 170, 171, 173, 175, 183
Presence (God's) 14, 143, 151
Prodigal Son 144
Prosphora 80
Psychoanalysis 25, 93, 154

'Rebecca' 74
Redemption 45f, 168
Religion 1, 12, 83
Repentance 115
Resurrection 135, 139, 167f, 170, 171, 174, 177, 184
Ritual 2, 3, 15, 16, 19, 21, 32, 36, 66, 105, 106, 115
Rivalry 5, 100, 139, 142, 143, 161
Rizutto, Anne-Marie 100
Role 75
Roman Catholic Church *see* Catholic Church
Rublev, Andrei 37
Russian Orthodox Church 127, 128

Sacks, Rabbi Jonathan 134
Saints 53f, 115, 148
'Sally' 56
Sagrada Familia 52f
Satan 98
Schism 127
School 18, 22, 32, 160

Schmemann, Father Alexander
Sentamu, Archbishop John 47
Sermon(s) 27, 25, 66ff, 92, 152, 158, 183
Sexual abuse 153
Sexual orientation 177f
Sexuality 60, 77, 158, 177
Sherine, Ariane 145
Sin 3, 46, 90, 163
Society 2, 4, 5, 11, 12, 49, 50, 72, 113, 151, 163, 175, 176, 182
    post-Christian 38
Soul 5, 16, 46, 53, 115
Spirit (Holy) 14, 28, 49, 105, 114, 154, 168f, 170f, 177; invocation of 46, 173, 182
Spiritual director 75
Spiritual renewal 172
Story, Christian 15, 50, 53, 61, 158, 165, 168
'Sue' 23
Suffering 17
Sunday school 21, 23, 184

Taizé 173
'Teresa' 20, 22, 53
'Tom' 153
Training (of clergy) 66f
Transubstantiation 123
Two natures of Christ 110f

Unity 29, 114, 115, 116, 120, 124, 127, 129, 132, 154, 181; quest for 180

Vermes, Pamela 111
Violence 5, 23, 99, 139, 146, 148
Vocation 22, 24, 77, 95, 152, 160, 162, 183
Voluntary work 70ff

Will (divine/human in Jesus) 146
Williams, Harry 5f
Williams, Archbishop Rowan 5
Witness 159, 166, 176ff
Worship 6, 7, 16, 17, 19, 24, 29, 30, 31, 36, 51, 82, 88, 89, 91, 108, 109, 115, 130, 132, 158, 166, 172, 175; multi-faith 134; offensive 157; prior to doctrine 170

Youth club 24